NARRATION OF CHINA

中国
社会建设
CHINA'S SOCIAL CONSTRUCTION

北京语言大学出版社
BEIJING LANGUAGE AND CULTURE
UNIVERSITY PRESS

用户必读

尊敬的用户：

在您使用本课件以前，请花少量时间阅读以下内容，相信这将极大地提升您讲座的效果。

《中国社会建设》是一套通用型讲座软件，结合中国社会建设领域的实际情况，从教育、就业、收入、社会保障、医疗卫生和社会治理等六个方面对中共十八届三中全会做了深入浅出的解读，勾勒出中国社会的图景和未来走向。本软件既适用于各国使馆人员、文化推广专员、中国社会研究者和教学者的讲授，也适用于关心中国社会建设和发展道路的海内外读者。

硬件配置：

由于《中国社会建设》课件内容丰富，包含了图片、动画、视频等大容量文件，因此它被保存在一张 DVD-ROM 的光盘中。如果想打开这个文件，您的计算机就必须具备播放 DVD-ROM 的光驱。其次，为了清晰而准确地展现内容，建议您使用有较高分辨率的投影仪。

软件配置：

您电脑的显示器分辨率不能低于 1024×768，否则您就看不到完整的课件界面了。您使用的操作系统也必须为以下几种：Windows XP, Windows vista, Windows 7, Windows 8。

使用步骤：

1. 这一条非常重要：在使用课件以前，请务必先阅读本手册中的全部正文内容。

《中国社会建设》课件的制作完全基于手册中的文稿，阅读正文内容是准确使用课件的前提，这部 5 万字左右的文稿也能带给您良好的阅读体验，并激发您讲座的灵感。

2. 如果您已经了解了全文内容，就可以对照着文稿和软件进行备课了。这本《指导手册》是您备课时的笔记和讲座中的讲义。

（1）文稿在页面的中间（❶），两边留出了一定的空间，供您做自己的讲课笔记（❷）。比如：本页的重点、计划使用的时间、软件里配套的多媒体资源，以及您的补充资料等等。

（2）《指导手册》首页上的按钮表可以帮助您熟悉课件的界面。

3. 使用中如果有疑问或建议，请发送邮件至 chinasketches@gmail.com，我们会为您解决疑难，或在以后的产品中进行完善。

现在，让我们打开《中国社会建设》课件，体验讲授带来的乐趣吧。

USER'S GUIDE

Dear User:

Before using the courseware, please read this page. We believe it will largely improve the effectiveness of your lecture.

China's Social Construction is a set of lecture software for general purpose. It offers a profound interpretation of the Third Plenary Session of the 18th CPC Central Committee in simple words from six aspects, namely, education, employment, income, social security, health care and social governance, sketching out a picture of the Chinese society and its future trends. This software applies not only to embassy staff, culture promotion commissioners, researchers and teachers of the Chinese society for teaching, but also to domestic and overseas readers who are concerned about China's social construction and development.

Hardware Requirements:

The courseware for *China's Social Construction* is rich in multi-media forms—pictures, cartoons, audios and videos as well as other large-capacity files, all on a DVD-ROM. To use the courseware, you need to equip your computer with a DVD-ROM drive. Besides, in order to have a clear and accurate presentation of the courseware, the use of a high-resolution projector is advisable.

Software Requirements:

The display resolution of your computer should be no less than 1024 × 768, otherwise you will be unable to see the complete user interface of the courseware. The courseware is supported in the following operating systems: Windows® XP, Windows® vista, or Windows® 7, Windows® 8.

Steps to Use:

1. This step is a very important! Before using the courseware, do please read the full text of the handbook.

The *China's Social Construction* courseware is entirely based on the handbook, and complete reading of the handbook is highly advisable before using the courseware. It

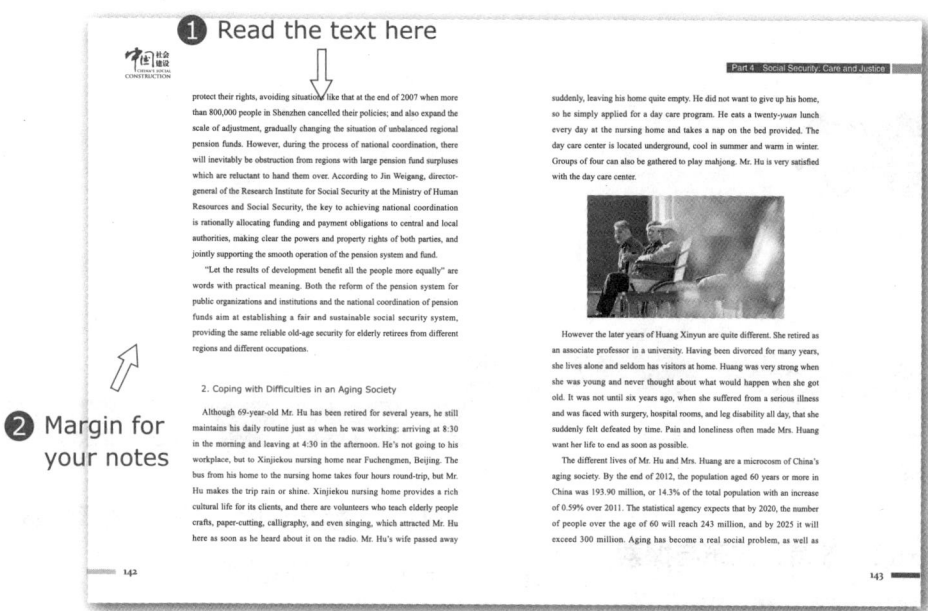

is hoped that the 50,000-word handbook will offer you a good reading experience and inspiration.

2. After thorough reading of the handbook, please get yourself familiar with the courseware in your hand, which will provide you with the notes for the preparation of your lessons.

(1) The text is shown in the middle of the page (❶), while margins are left on the two sides for your notes (❷), such as the key points, your time plan, the multi-media resources of the courseware or other teaching materials.

(2) The button list on the first page of the handbook will help you get familiar with the courseware interface.

3. Should you have any other difficulties and suggestions in the use of the courseware, please send us e-mails to chinasketches@gmail.com and we will reply to you as soon as possible. Your advice and suggestions are highly appreciated.

Now, let's start our pleasant journey while learning *China's Social Construction*!

目 录

001-037

前言 ... 1

第一章　教育：改革与探索　2
第一节　促进教育公平　3
第二节　改革招生制度　6
第三节　鼓励社会力量办学　9

第二章　就业：促进与保障　14
第一节　促进社会就业　15
第二节　鼓励个人创业　18
第三节　保障劳动权利　22

第三章　收入：保护与调节　26
第一节　规范分配秩序　27
第二节　减轻个税负担　30
第三节　缩小收入差距　33

038-067

第四章　社会保障：关怀与公平　38
第一节　统筹养老保险　39
第二节　应对老龄难题　42
第三节　安居才能安心　46
第四节　完善农村社会保障　50

第五章　医疗卫生：根基与安全　54
第一节　建设全民医保　55
第二节　完善医疗服务体系　59
第三节　鼓励社会办医　62
第四节　调整生育政策　64

068-081

第六章　社会治理：创新与和谐　68
第一节　改进治理方式　69
第二节　激发社会活力　72
第三节　正确处理矛盾　75
第四节　保障公共安全　79

082-119

Preface 82

**Part 1 Education:
Reform and Exploration**
84
1. Promoting Educational Equality   85
2. Reforming the Enrollment System   90
3. Encouraging Private Education   95

**Part 2 Employment:
Promotion and
Guarantee**   102
1. Promoting Social Employment   103
2. Encouraging Entrepreneurship   108
3. Protecting Labor Rights   114

120-157

**Part 3 Income:
Protection and
Regulation**   120
1. Standardizing the Income
Distribution Pattern   121
2. Reducing the Individual Tax
Burden   126
3. Narrowing the Income Gap   130

**Part 4 Social Security:
Care and Justice**   136
1. Coordinating Retirement Pensions   137
2. Coping with Difficulties in an
Aging Society   142
3. Housing is Primary for Settlement   148
4. Improving Social Security in Rural
Areas   154

CONTENTS

158-177

Part 5   Healthcare: Foundation and Security   158

1. Establishing Nationwide Healthcare   159
2. Improving the Medical Service System   166
3. Encouraging Private Investment in the Medical Sector   169
4. Improving the Family Planning Policy   174

178-199

Part 6   Social Governance: Innovation and Harmony   178

1. Improving Governance Methods   179
2. Stimulating Social Vitality   184
3. Properly Handling Contradictions   189
4. Protecting Public Safety   195

前　言

英国著名的历史学家阿诺德·约瑟夫·汤因比曾说："几千年来，中国人比世界上任何民族都成功地把几亿民众从政治、文化上团结起来。他们显示出这种在政治、文化上统一的本领，具有无与伦比的成功经验。"中国社会就是在这种团结和统一的基础上形成的共同体，它常常有赖于政治层面统一的制度设计和自上而下的推动以实现发展变迁。这一点已经得到历史证明，也是认识中国社会不可或缺的视角。

1978年中共十一届三中全会以来，"改革开放"政策使中国经济社会的面貌发生了巨大变化，成就了全球瞩目的发展奇迹。但快速发展也带来诸多亟待解决的问题。2012年中国共产党第十八次全国代表大会进行了换届选举。新一届领导集体的执政思路是什么？改革下一步怎么走？所有人的目光聚焦在中国共产党第十八届三中全会上。2013年11月12日，中共十八届三中全会审议通过了《中共中央关于全面深化改革若干重大问题的决定》(文内均简称《决定》)，对中国未来十年的改革开放和发展作出了纲领性规划。《决定》提出，要站在新的历史起点上全面深化改革，并对加快发展社会主义市场经济、民主政治、先进文化、和谐社会和生态文明作出顶层设计，为中国未来的改革道路指明了方向。

具体到社会建设领域，《决定》的布局是，紧紧围绕更好保障和改善民生、促进社会公平正义深化社会体制改革，改革收入分配制度，促进共同富裕，推进社会领域制度创新，推进基本公共服务均等化，加快形成科学有效的社会治理体制，确保社会既充满活力又和谐有序。如果说"和谐有序"是中共十六届四中全会提出的"和谐社会"目标的基本内涵，"充满活力"的提法则表明社会自我调节的功能得到政府前所未有的重视，它作为连结政治、经济、文化、生态文明的有机体将在未来发挥更大的积极作用，在动态运行中实现和谐。

无论是"充满活力"还是"和谐有序"的提法，都具有强烈的现实针对性。改革开放三十多年来，中国在全球化加速的背景下同时经历经济转轨和社会转型。在从计划经济向市场经济转轨、由传统农业社会向现代工业社会和信息社会转型的过程中，社会结构、利益格局、社会心态、社会管理等都发生了巨大变化。社会在进步的同时也不可避免地出现了一些矛盾，潜藏着一定的运行风险。它们既是社会转型带来的结果，也构成下一步社会建设的起点。

《中国社会建设》对《决定》中关于社会事业改革和社会治理体制创新的议题做了深入浅出的解读，在讲述方式上回避大而全的视角，结合中国社会建设领域的实际情况，勾勒出直接清晰而易于理解的中国社会图景和未来走向。在破题上，《中国社会建设》采取关键词描述的方式，把主题分解成教育、就业、收入、社会保障、医疗卫生和社会治理六大领域共21个关键词，每个关键词从中国社会生活中的具体案例切入，展现中国政府以渐进方式推动社会建设改革的历程，并解析相关配套政策措施的走向，以点带面，述论结合，兼顾广度与深度，便于国际社会认识与理解。

第一章　教育：改革与探索

　　中国有句古话，"十年树木，百年树人"，意指教育是一项关系社会发展的长期事业。重视教育是中国自古至今的传统。1949年中华人民共和国成立后，政府大力发展教育事业，改变了过去文盲率高达80%的状况，大幅度提升了中国国民的科学文化素质，为中国参与国际竞争提供了人才基础。

　　然而在长期的发展中，教育领域也积累了一些弊端。教育资源整体上还不够丰富，不同地区和人群可获得的教育资源和教育机会不够均衡，"一考定终身"的考试模式常常受到社会舆论的质疑，社会力量办学在教育领域仍未能够得到充分的施展。

　　不过，中国政府已经充分认识到这些弊端，教育改革的必要性在社会上也有着广泛的共识。因材施教，让每一个人都得到教育的机会，让每一个人都成为有用的人才，这是教育改革的理想。中国未来的教育将回归以人为本的轨道，不断改革与探索。

第一节　促进教育公平

"如果不能在这里参加高考,我只能选择回老家再复读一年。"曾经忧心忡忡的谢福乐如今无需再为高考发愁。当班主任徐丹告诉他明年可以在安徽就地高考的消息时,他终于松了一口气,可以毫无负担地投入复习了。与谢福乐同样幸运的还有福建女孩伍艳群。伍艳群在南京读书,因为无法在江苏参加高考,这些年她曾辗转三次回到老家。当她获悉2013年可以像其他当地考生一样在南京参加高考时,一颗悬着的心终于放下了。谢福乐和伍艳群们有一个共同的名字——异地高考生。2013年异地高考政策放开后,各地首批异地高考生将同本地考生一起走进考场,追逐他们的"大学梦"。

中国近几年对高考改革和准许异地高考的呼声很高。在2012年"两会(全国人民代表大会和中国人民政治协商会议)"期间,全国9万多名随迁子女家长就共同发布了《公开信》。公开信指出,当前全国已有2.6亿流动人口,其背后是5800万留守儿童和2700万随迁子女。2013年统计数据显示,全国义务教育阶段在校生中进城务工人员随迁子女共1393.87万人。"异地高考"问题已经到了不得不解决的阶段。2012年3月山东省率先突破高考户籍限制,允许外地考生参加山东高考。2013年9月北京教育部门公布《2014年进城务工人员随迁子女在京参加高等职业学校招生考试实施办法》,继2013年来京务工人员随迁

子女在京可以参加中等职业学校招生录取后，2014年起逐步放开随迁子女在京参加高等职业学校招生录取。广东省随迁子女在广东报名参加高考的"新政"也将于2014年启动。截至2013年11月，除西藏表示将在年内出台方案外，其余参加高考的30省（区、市）均已公布了异地高考方案。异地高考政策的出台，与十八届三中全会指出的"大力促进教育公平"的目标是完全一致的。

关于教育公平，全会还指出，应"健全家庭经济困难学生资助体系，构建利用信息化手段扩大优质教育资源覆盖面的有效机制，逐步缩小区域、城乡、校际差距"。北京航空航天大学能源与动力工程学院2013级本科生国杰就是国家健全家庭经济困难学生资助体系政策的受益人。来自西藏的国杰家中有9人，劳动力仅3人，年收入3000元左右，他只身一人坐了45个小时的火车硬座，怀揣不到300元来到北京，辅导员帮助他通过"绿色通道"办理报到手续，并顺利入学，学校还为他免费提供被褥、脸盆、热水瓶等生活用品，让他充分感受到了温暖。近年来，各地高校在助力贫困学生方面都颇为用心，高校家庭经济困难学生正在日益完善的国家助学体系中安心求学。北京大学每年推出"燕园关爱助学金"，将资金提前发到新生银行卡中，解决学生入学的路费和生活费。中国人民大学为贫困新生打造了一条包括快速办理入学手续、发放免费餐卡、为特困新生发放自行车及卧具、现场办理新生保险、现场受理奖励性贷学金申请等多种方式在内的"绿色通道"。西安交通大学全校每年约有70%的学生获得各类奖（助）学金，总金额达5100余万元。学校每年还为家庭经济困难学生发放临时困难补助等约300万元。

未来，健全家庭经济困难学生资助体系将是中国教育事业改革继续坚持的重点方向。教育部教育发展研究中心主任张力解释说，"在下一步教育改革中，要有效结合全国社会征信体系和个人收入信息系统建设，拓宽家庭经济困难本科高职学生资助渠道，让每个孩子都能成为有用之才"。张力同时也指出，伴随信息化进程的加快，需要更加完善教育信息网络对城乡各级各类学校和教育机构的覆盖，不断创新大规模网络学习模式，建设与国家教育现代化目标相适应的教育信息化体系。

在与教育公平有关的话题里，"择校热"是长期困扰基础教育领域的难题，且由于各种主客观原因，改革成效一直以来都不显著。32.5万元不是个小数目，但在北京市景山东街，32.5万元只可以买到一平米的学区房。而如此高价是因为这里能上"北京最牛小学"实验二小。为了让孩子能上一所名校，家长"南征北战"，帮孩子报名参加各种择校考试。

选择学校其实就是选择老师，师资是义务教育均衡发展的关键。一直以来，好教师往优质学校流动的现象较为普遍，加之教育资源分配不均，各地均存在设重点学校、重点班的现象。《决定》提到的"统筹城乡义务教育资源均衡配置，实行公办学校标准化建设和校长教师交流轮岗"可以看成是破解择校难题的一条可行之路。事实上，从中央到地方，各级政府一直致力于缩小城乡之间、校际之间义务教育师资水平的差距。早在1999年，《中共中央、国务院关于深化教育改革全面推进素质教育的决定》中就做出了相关规定，以此推动城镇学校教师、乡村教师的流动，提高义务教育学校的教育水平。2010年国家

教育规划纲要和 2012 年《国务院关于加强教师队伍建设的意见》更将教师资源的流动细则做了明确规定。截至 2013 年 8 月底，已有 22 个省（区、市）出台了关于教师流动的相关政策，通过支教、对口支援、走教制度等途径和方式推进教师校长交流。例如，北京市通过建立名师工作室、导师团、名师讲座、跨校送课、师徒结对等形式实现优质教师资源的共享辐射。再如，湖南省建立乡镇音、体、美教师无校籍制度，全县农村学校音、体、美教师只聘任到乡镇，不定点到校，对村小、教学点的音、体、美教学实行走教制。

要想搬开石头，实现教育的公平，没有别的办法，唯有深化改革。教育部副部长刘利民表示，按照《决定》，教育部将推出义务教育免试就近入学，试行学区制和九年一贯对口招生制度，义务教育制度学校将不设重点学校、重点班。教育部已经制定了《关于进一步做好小学升初中免试就近入学工作的实施意见》。对于择校问题突出的 19 个重点大城市，教育部将坚持一市一案的工作方针，抓热点学校、抓关键环节、抓重点时段，完善相关政策，努力破解择校难题。新的、更合理的利益格局立起来，旧的利益格局才会真正倒塌。在教育改革的蓝图完成之际，相信择校热会逐渐成为历史。

第二节 改革招生制度

"去香港的主要原因并非奖学金，而是希望能多了解香港，尝试不一样的教育体制。香港高校更加开放和自由，设置更加前沿，更加国际化。"选择香港大学的北京文科状元梁倩这样描述她心目中的"完美高校"。香港大学公布的 2013—2014 学年内地本科生录取结果显示，当年该校共接到 12513 名内地考生申请。而在最终录取的 303 名考生中，包括 16 名内地高考省市"状元"。香港理工大学该年度也吸引近 4000 名内地考生报考。香港院校近年来持续吸引内地优质生源，不少考生更是舍弃清华、北大等内地顶尖名校而选择赴港就学。香港高校备受青睐让不少人借机反思内地现行的招生制度。

当然，改革招生制度不是一朝一夕的事情，教育部门近些年也一直在探索新的招生制度和模式，高校自主招生就是其中颇具代表性的模式。高校自主招生又叫高校自主选拔录取改革试点，于2003年正式启动。根据教育部2012年《关于进一步深化高校自主选拔录取改革试点工作的指导意见》，自主招生主要面向具有学科特长和创新潜质的优秀学生，以面试为主考查学生的素质和能力，笔试科目一般不超过两门。各个高校在自主招生的改革之路上也是摸索不断。回顾2013年自主选拔，最明显的变化是淡化"综合素质"，强调"学科特色"。对考生而言，则是笔试科目减少，面试权重增加。有专家指出，教育部此举出于两方面考虑：一是针对自主选拔成为"小高考"并加重学生负担的社会舆论做出反馈；二是要求高校进一步明确自己的选材标准，有的放矢，缩小考试规模，提升人才选拔效率。

进入2013年11月，随着清华大学公布特殊自主招生"领军计划"实施办法、北京大学"中学校长实名推荐"资质认定结束，2014年高校自主招生陆续启动。尽管"北约（北京大学等13所重点高校）"、"华约（清华大学等7所重点高校）"、"卓越（北京理工大学等9所重点高校）"等高校自主招生联盟尚未发布2014年自招的具体测试办法，但除了往年的笔试、面试外，更多的高校开始采取"科学营"、"金秋营"、"体验营"等形式，在活动中对学生进行测试，通过者给予自主招生资格或自主招生优惠，试图以更多元化的渠道自主选拔学生。在北京大学举办的"2013全国优秀中学生'百年数学'科学体验营"中，参加体验营的山东考生陈硕对最后的测试心里没底："写成语太难了，很多题都没答上，完全是'神题'啊！"而且他提到，在综合笔试环节，还有一道题目给出四个图形，需要考生推理出第五个图形，与公务员行政能力测试的题目类似。清华大学招办主任于涵表示，基于学科方向来选拔人才和设计考核环节将是自主招考未来的发展方向。

各高校在自主招生改革上为什么要下这么大的功夫呢？因为高考对中国人而言意义重大。多年来，中考、高考这两大考试基本上与每一个中国孩子的成长与命运都息息相关，所谓"一考定终身"，两大考试的

任何动向都会牵动民众的神经,成为关注的焦点。2013年10月21日北京市教育考试院公布了中高考改革方案。其中,降低中高考英语分值、提高语文分值,重点高中名额向一般中学倾斜等成为方案的亮点。2016年实施的新高考方案则将对考试内容、试卷结构、考试科目的分值进行调整。届时,高考文史类、理工类总分仍为750分,但语文由150分增至180分,数学仍为150分,英语由150分减为100分,明显加重了语文科目的分值,降低了英语的比重。同时,高考将实行社会化考试,一年两次考试,学生可多次参加,按最好成绩计入高考总分,成绩三年内有效。另外值得关注的是,2010年,教育部等五部委发布《关于调整部分高考加分项目和进一步加强管理工作的通知》,规范高考加分等相关问题。从2014年起,只有国际奥林匹克竞赛的参赛者才有保送生资格,全国奥林匹克竞赛一、二、三等奖的获奖者不再具有保送资格,省级奥林匹克竞赛一等奖的获得者不再具有保送和加分资格。

在以上这些考试及招生改革基础上,《决定》给教育考试招生制度提出了更明确的思路和更高的要求。教育部部长袁贵仁在解析有关考试招生制度的内容时认为,考试招生制度是教育领域综合改革"牵一发而动全身"的重点领域和关键环节。"探索招生和考试相对分离、学生考试多次选择、学校依法自主招生、专业机构组织实施、政府宏观管理、社会参与监督的运行机制"是改革的方向。所以,一方面,就考试招生制度而言,在全国统考中要逐步探索减少科目、不分文理科、外语采取社会化考试一年多考的路子，特别还要试行普通高校、高职院校、成人高校之间的学分转换，拓宽终身学习的通道；另一方面，在改革考试招生制度的同时，也要推行初高中学业水平考试和综合素质评价，逐步建立普通高校基于统一高考和高中学业水平考试成绩的综合评价多元录取机制。教育部副部长刘利民透露，在总体方案的框架下，教育部将陆续出台包括小升初、高中学业水平考试、中考和高考改革办法等多个配套实施意见。例如高中学业水平考试将主要考查学生高中学业完成情况，分别采用合格和等级方式来呈现考试成绩，不再用百分制，避免"分分计较"。学生也将根据自己的兴趣、志向和优势，自觉选择部分等级性考试科目来参加，每一门课程学完即考，"一门一清"，避免毕业时"一次考三年"的压力。

《决定》所体现的顶层设计以及后续跟进配套政策，应该是教育改革中系统性与综合性最强的一次。其目的就是为了真正扭转应试教育千军万马过独木桥的现状，通过深度推进，从根本上解决"一考定终身"的弊端，为亿万学生提供多样化的学习选择和成长途径，科学选拔人才，维护社会公平，彰显有教无类、因材施教的理念，搭建起符合中国国情的人才成长"立交桥"。

第三节 鼓励社会力量办学

"卡梅拉就和别的小鸡不一样，它总是想去看海，总是想照顾可怜的小黑猫，总是想……""鼠小弟就和别的老鼠不一样，它总是想给大象哥哥穿小背心，总是想学长颈鹿摘苹果，总是想……"课堂里传出的不是老师的讲课声或沙沙的笔记声，而是学生正在朗诵这些美妙的故事，畅谈自己对故事的理解。在这里，阅读是教学的核心。每一个孩子在整个小学和中学阶段都要阅读上千本绘本、两百多部文学著作，还要演出几十部儿童剧，写诗，作画，聆听音乐，感受自我价值。这里是新教育实验小学，目前它已成为民间探索中小学教育改革的一个典型。

而另一个民办教育的典型则是新东方教育集团。它已在全国50座

城市设立了57所学校、700多家学习中心、7家产业机构、32家书店，年发行图书1200万册，累计面授学员1600多万人次，改变了一拨又一拨学生的命运。2013年9月新东方集团创始人俞敏洪成为耿丹学院理事长，新东方以间接方式进入民办大学学历教育领域。

新教育和新东方正是中国民间力量参与教育的缩影，而民办教育的发展则是中国改革开放进程的一个缩影。民办教育的壮大与国家的成长是一种良性互动，破译二者之间的关系也是读懂中国的一个切入点。1987年教育部颁布《关于社会力量办学的若干暂行规定》，中国的民办教育开始有法可依。1997年国务院颁布《社会力量办学条例》，鼓励社会力量举办实施义务教育的教育机构作为国家实施义务教育的补充，但当时依然严格控制社会力量举办高等教育机构。2002年12月，全国人大通过《民办教育促进法》，国家将民办教育事业纳入了国民经济和社会发展规划，国家保障民办学校的办学自主权。至此，民办学校与公办学校终于具有了同等的法律地位。2010年《国家中长期教育改革和发展规划纲要（2010-2020年）》指出，要积极探索营利性和非营利性民办学校分类管理，并提出"支持民办学校创新体制机制和育人模式，提高质量，办出特色，办好一批高水平民办学校"。2012年出台《关于鼓励和引导民间资金进入教育领域促进民办教育健康发展的实施意见》，在教育系统内部落实了民办学校与公办学校的同等待遇。2013年9月，国务院法制办公室就《教育法律一揽子修订草案(征求意见稿)》向社会公开征求意见,根据《征求意见稿》,在《民办教育促进法》第五条中增加规定,民办学校与公办学校具有同等法律地位,并按照其法人属性享受相应优惠政策。

  为了在实践上更切实推进民办教育改革,教育部从2011年开始在全国各地开展了12项改革试点。浙江温州开展非营利性和营利性民办学校分类管理改革试点,出台了各种相应的政策,三年里共吸引了45亿元社会资金。期间,全国23个省份均出台了促进民办教育发展的政策措施,据不完全统计,共吸引500多亿元社会资金进入教育领域。社会力量办教育正在逐步成长壮大,成为中国教育事业的重要组成部分。教育部副部长鲁昕于2013年12月3日发表署名文章《推进民办教育健康发展》中指出,全国各级各类民办学校达14万所,在校生人数3911万。民办教育在各级教育的在校生比例,学前教育达50%,普通小学为6%,普通初中为10%,中等职业学校为11%,普通高中为10%,高等教育为22%。社会力量办教育在丰富教育资源供给、提供多元选择、缓解财政压力、激发教育活力等方面发挥了重要作用。

  《决定》明确要求"深化教育领域综合改革",特别提出要"健全政府补贴、政府购买服务、助学贷款、基金奖励、捐资激励等制度,鼓励社会力量兴办教育"。可以说,作为教育事业重要组成部分的民办教育迎来了更好的发展机遇。教育部副部长鲁昕认为,促进社会力量办教育,要充分发挥市场对民办教育资源配置的作用。一方面,政府要为民间资金兴办教育创造良好条件,充分调动社会力量办学兴教的积极性;另一方面,民办学校也要密切关注市场需要和群众需求,特别是民办高等院校和职业学校,要按照区域产业发展设置和调整专业。

  鼓励社会兴办教育,需要政策、体制、社会等多个层面协同推进。从政策层面上,政府对社会力量办教育要予以积极支持,探索各类办学主体通过独资、合资、合作、股份制等多种方式举办民办教育。同时政府补贴也要及时、到位,对民办教育机构在学校建设、学生培养、教师培训、贷款融资等方面给予经费补助。从学校管理体制上,要允许学校管理者、骨干教师等以知识、技术、管理、资本等多种方式参与办学，鼓励民办学校师生创造的专利等成果经评估后成为学校的出资。同时，要对民办学校进行分类管理。分类管理是民办教育健康发展的重要保障，也是世界各国的普遍做法。教育规划纲要提出了"积极探索营利性和非营利性民办学校分类管理"，并在此基础上进行了分类管理改革的试点。从社会层面上，政府要鼓励行业、企业等社会力量参与公办学校办学，也要鼓励公办学校与民办学校之间通过相互购买服务等多种方式互相支持，合作办学。

在享有一系列利好政策的同时，民办学校应探索更好的发展管理模式，破解制约民办教育自身发展的体制机制障碍。例如，对于民办学校中较为突出的家族式、家长式、经验式管理所带来的弊端，就需要健全法人治理结构，完善董事会、监事会制度，规范董事会、监事会的职责和运行。落实民办学校招生、收费、课程、管理等方面的办学自主权，保障民办学校依法依规独立自主的发展空间。客观上讲，目前中国社会总体上对民办教育的认可度还未达到良好预期水平，因而，加快建设一批具有引领示范作用的高水平、有特色的民办学校，引导民办学校狠抓内涵建设，不断提高办学质量和特色势在必行。教育部副部长鲁昕对此也提出，政府下一步会加快建立非营利性民办高校联盟的进程，搭建高水平民办高校示范平台，将一批坚持非营利办学，定位准、管理好、质量优的民办高校组织起来，树立民办教育的良好形象。

《**决定**》对社会力量兴办教育的新部署是教育改革发展迈进的一大步，同时也为社会兴办教育提供了良好的机遇和广阔的空间。政策支持的大门已经打开，社会力量办学正在全力加速。但在昂首阔步之时，社会办学力量需要同时加强责任意识和进取意识，才能走上良性发展的轨道。

第二章　就业：促进与保障

回顾世界历史上几次重大的经济危机，都能看到这样的场景：等待救济发放的队伍一眼望不到头，失业者脸上写满忧愁和焦虑。在任何一个时代和社会，就业都是民生之本。如果劳动者不能实现充分就业，社会必然潜伏着巨大的风险。

中国是世界上人口最多的国家，也是就业压力最大的国家。经济的高速发展固然为社会持续提供着就业岗位，但劳动力市场的供需矛盾依然十分突出，这已成为中国当下和今后相当长一个时期内的矛盾焦点。新增就业人口、城镇下岗失业人群、农村转移剩余劳动力构成中国就业大军的三大主力，他们能否顺利找到工作、实现就业，影响着中国社会的稳定和发展。

中国政府对此做了大量努力，不断拓宽就业渠道，增加就业岗位，鼓励个人创业，并对民营经济和中小微企业的发展给予扶持。而与劳动相关的各类法律法规的出台，在提升社会就业率的同时也在不断提高着就业质量。

第一节 促进社会就业

早上九点,陈雷紧攥着用心撰写的简历,准时来到武汉市纳杰人才市场的招聘会现场。陈雷在师范学院学习心理学,尽管学习成绩不错,实习经历丰富,沟通能力也好,但在求职路上却屡屡碰壁,不是投出去的简历石沉大海,就是一路过关斩将最终倒在面试环节。刚开始求职时,他还期待着一份月薪 2000—3000 元、准点上下班、正常休假的工作。而现在,只要有公司肯录用自己,职位也能胜任,陈雷就谢天谢地了。同班同学的情况也不乐观,43 个人里只有不到一半落实了工作。这些 2013 年即将走出校门的大学生与全国 699 万应届生一道面临着就业考验。

事实上,陈雷每天乘坐地铁时,移动电视里都会发布很多工作信息。这些大多是保安、保洁、家政等服务性工作,陈雷觉得并不适合自己。而远在深圳的陈垂完对自己从事的保洁工作却很满意。她五年前从原单位下岗,上有老下有小的家庭一下子变得捉襟见肘起来。只有中专文化、年龄也偏大的陈垂完想要再找一份工作非常困难。蛇口区招商街道办事处劳动保障所在走访中了解到她的失业情况,推荐她去一家清洁服务公司做保洁员。由于岗前培训积极,工作表现也很出色,陈垂完随后就被派到街道办事处食堂负责做饭与场地卫生。虽说保洁工作比较辛苦,陈垂完却很珍惜这份来之不易的工作。

无论是陈雷还是陈垂完,都是中国庞大的就业"大军"里的一员。据相关部门估算,除去699万高校应届毕业生,2013年全国还有2500万城镇劳动力需要实现就业。再加上大量的农村转移剩余劳动力,中国的就业人口规模几乎相当于2012年加拿大全国约3488万的人口总数。考虑到宏观经济增速放缓、产业转型升级的大背景,中国就业市场的供需矛盾压力空前增大。

在巨大的就业压力下,上至中央政府下至各省市都出台了一系列促进就业的政策。针对大学生普遍青睐一线城市、大型国企和机关公务员导致的结构性求职与用工困难,国务院办公厅在《关于做好2013年全国普通高等学校毕业生就业工作的通知》中采取双管齐下的办法,一方面通过社保补贴、培训补贴等经济手段加大对小微企业的扶持力度,鼓励其吸纳大学生就业;另一方面积极引导大学生转变就业观念,在民营企业、非公有制经济组织和城乡基层公共管理岗位等用人需求中寻找就业机会。根据规定,中小微企业当年每新招用一名应届高校毕业生,签订1年以上期限劳动合同并按规定缴纳社会保险的,可以享受国家一次性给予的1000元补贴;属于小微型企业的还给予1年期限的社保补贴。各地方政府也不断加大"三支一扶"(支教、支农、支医和扶贫)、"大学生村官计划"、"大学生志愿服务西部计划"等基层就业政策的宣传与实施力度,引导大学生前往最需要知识与技术的农村地区、西部地区发挥自己的价值。而对在离校之时仍未实现就业的高校毕业生,国务院则组织实施"离校未就业高校毕业生就业促进计划",由各地公共就业人才服务机构对这一群体进行实名登记,以提供用人信息、组织创业培训、开展就业见习等方式落实一对一就业帮扶,帮助他们在年底前实现就业或参加到就业准备活动中。

一对一帮扶同时也是政府解决城镇就业困难人员实现再就业的政策经验。当前,城镇就业困难人员实现再就业一般由各地方政府根据当地实际统一规划安排。首先是对就业困难人员进行界定,在各地的不同政策中基本都包括大龄、残疾、享受最低生活保障、军烈属、单亲家庭抚养未成年子女等情况的失业人员。然后由各地公共就业服务机构或街道办事处对符合条件的就业困难人员进行实名登记管理，掌握他们的就业愿望、求职意向、家庭生活等情况，并制定出个性化的援助方案，采取职业培训、岗位见习、推荐录用等多种方式与用人单位对接。为了保证援助的实际效果，不少地方的就业服务机构或街道办在困难人员实现再就业后还会组织定期的跟踪回访，调查用人单位和援助对象双方的意见，从而能对劳动力资源进行更为合理的调配。陈垂完就是深圳市就业帮扶政策的受益者，而根据深圳市人力资源和社会保障局公布的相关数据，2012年全市帮扶就业困难人员实现就业24529人；2013年前三季度失业转就业人数则已达到24071人。

正如中国国家主席习近平2013年8月到基层考察时指出的那样，就业是永恒的课题，更是世界性难题。中国每年新增1000多万就业人口，直接关系到经济社会的可持续发展与长期稳定，因此，必须大力促进就业创业。《决定》提出，要建立经济发展和扩大就业的联动机制，健全政府促进就业的责任制度。2013年，经济增速放缓导致的各行各业用人需求下降与空前的毕业生规模共同制造了就业市场巨大的供需缺口，同样的局面在2008年全球金融危机时也出现过。如何在调整经济结构、实现经济转型升级的战略下增强就业市场抵御经济相对下行风险的能力，构建更为合理、稳定、安全的经济与就业联动机制，就成为政府促进就业责任制度的题中之义，因为劳动者实现就业不仅是个体的市场行为，同时也属于政府公共管理的范畴。习近平主席考察时提出"集中精力抓发展"、"把就业再就业工作做实"、"劳动者要转变观念"的三点要求就表明了经济与就业、政府与劳动者在就业问题上的关联。《决定》把发展尤其是经济发展作为解决社会问题的根本和关键，这就为促进社会就业、稳定民生民心提供了最大的保障。

在就业政策走向上，政府将根据不同的就业群体和就业需求进行有针对性的制度设计。如对陈雷这样的高校毕业生，将运用市场和行政两种力量，一方面结合产业升级开发更多适合大学生的就业岗位，另一方面由政府出面购买基层公共管理和社会服务岗位，吸纳大学生就业。可以预见，类似"三支一扶"、"村官计划"等就业扶持工程还将进一步加

大实施力度和覆盖范围,并通过提高劳动待遇和社会福利增加基层工作对大学生的吸引力。例如北京市2013年大学生"村官"因普涨约一倍工资,待遇基本与公务员齐平,所以吸引了1.6万名大学毕业生竞争2400个"村官"名额,整体竞争从去年的2.9:1猛增到6.6:1。城镇就业困难人员则是另一个政策扶持重点,像陈垂完这样的失业人员最需要的就是公共就业服务体系的帮助以及必要的失业保障和劳动培训。中国还将完善城乡均等的公共就业创业服务体系,构建劳动者终身职业培训体系,进一步发挥基层就业服务机构在落实促进就业政策、扩大社会就业方面的作用。在预防失业、促进就业方面,政府也将逐步完善就业失业监测统计制度。2013年的就业困难没有难住上海,一定程度上就归功于上海市首创的就业失业预警体系。这一体系至少囊括三种数据对比,即所有企业的招退工数据实时统计、企业在上海人才市场发布的招聘职位和求职登记总数以及大规模的企业减员,政府再根据这些数据有针对性地制定政策。例如,2012年启动的"启航计划"就解决了上海一批长期失业青年的就业问题。

就业是民生之本,社会实现多层次、可持续的充分就业格局,既是经济增长强大的助推器,又是提高人民生活水平的根本途径。中共十八届三中全会把发展和改革都统一到增进人民福祉的落脚点上,以此来谋划、实施促进社会就业的各项政策,凝聚民心与共识,聚合市场与政府,将有信心面对任何就业难题的考验。

第二节 鼓励个人创业

2013年9月24日是黄亦楠的大日子,她正式从北京市工商局海淀分局领回了营业执照。历经两个多月的辛苦奔波,这个刚上大学三年级的女孩终于迈过了创业路上最重要的坎儿。为了办理注册登记新公司的手续,黄亦楠过去两个月里总共跑了两趟社保局、七趟工商局、两趟中关村科技园区服务中心办事大厅、一趟国税局和两趟地税局,填了不下50份表格。营业执照到手后,她才如释重负地长舒了一口气。

就在半年前，比黄亦楠高一届的师兄师姐们正面临"最难就业年"的考验。为了解决全国699万高校毕业生的就业问题，从中央到地方各级政府都出台了各种应对政策，尤其鼓励大学生放开"求职"思维，选择自主创业。但摆在黄亦楠面前的行政审批程序过于繁杂，大大增加了创业时间和经济成本，对创业者的积极性形成了不小的打击。创业者们感到最头疼的往往是行政审批程序这道门槛。李克强总理在地方调研的时候经常听到基层反映，办个事、创个业要盖几十个公章，群众对此意见很大。由此，政府主动简政放权，为创业者打开方便之门、提供优质的公共服务，就成为深化行政审批制度改革的重点。

在江苏宿迁市经营广告公司的朱海涛就切实体会到了政府简政放权的好处。在过去一年里，宿迁对全市200多项行政审批项目进行了逐条审查，先后召开各类座谈会90余场，分析每一个审批项目设立的可行性和必要性。审查人员发现，一些审批项目超过三年都没有行使过，已经形同虚设；一些项目用得特别多，效果并不好；还有些项目手续繁杂，束缚了市场的发展，比如气象局对氢气球的管理就直接影响到朱海涛。他的广告公司有一项业务是在各种庆典活动上放氢气球，而施放的时间、地点、数量、人员等都必须报气象局审批。为此朱海涛必须天天跑气象局，有时候还因为审批时间过长，客户等不及，不得不中止合作。宿迁市经过评估和考察，认为管理氢气球关键在"放"，气球易燃易爆的安全隐患可以通过加强施放人员的培训和现场监管力度来解决，于是暂停了气象局事前审批手续。现在，朱海涛再也不用天天跑气象局了。

经过简政放权和各项改革调整，宿迁市一级审批事项压减了136项，只剩下57项。在宿迁的便民行政服务大厅，市政府各部门都派驻了工作人员，按"一窗式"流程为市民提供便捷服务。创业者只需从综合窗口递送一次申请材料，填一次表格，相关信息就会录入网络平台，工商、质监、国税、地税等各部门可以同时查阅材料、同时审批。曾女士前天刚刚递交了注册公司所需的材料，第二天下午就领到了开办公司所需的所有证照。而按照改革之前的审批流程，一个个证照拿下来最快也得一两周。宿迁市改革行政审批制度既方便了朱海涛这样的私营企业主开展日常业务，也节约了曾女士这样的创业者注册登记的时间，极大地提高了行政服务效率。

除了改革行政审批制度，政府针对创业者资本不足的实际，也从税收上减轻其经营负担。由于资本和人力的局限，创业者们进入市场往往选择从投入不多、规模不大的小微企业做起。2013年7月24日，国务院常务会议规定，从8月1日起对小微企业中月销售额不超过两万元的增值税小规模纳税人和营业税纳税人，暂免征收增值税和营业税。按照这一政策，一个月销售额两万元的小微企业每月可以免掉600元的税额，一年下来就是7200元。小微企业利润普遍不高，以10%的利润率估算，一个月的利润也才2000元，免征部分的税额相当于为企业实实在在挣回了将近4个月的利润。对更多准备进入市场的创业者而言，这也是在释放更加积极的政策信号。税负减轻意味着市场效益的相对提高，有利于创业者更加精细地衡量创业风险，结合市场需求和国家鼓励创业的政策导向，形成更加合理成熟的创业方案。

创业是激发市场活力、带动社会就业的重要手段。《决定》提出，完善扶持创业的优惠政策，形成政府激励创业、社会支持创业、劳动者勇于创业的新机制。改革行政审批制度和切实减轻小微企业税负都是这个新机制的一部分，政府通过这样的新机制不断放手，让创业者能够顺利进入市场，顺利经营业务，顺利提高收益。可以预见的是，行政审批制度改革的力度还会加大，范围还会扩展。以广东省为例，2012年国务院就批准广东省作为改革行政审批制度的先行试点，为在全国范围内推进行政审批制度改革积累经验。一年后，广东省在第一批改革项目目录中明确取消179项，转移55项，下放实施115项，委托管理5项，四个类别的调整共计354项，占改革之前实际审批项目的1/3以上。如此大刀阔斧的改革，直接受益的就是珠三角地区的民营经济和众多创业者，而广东经验也会在未来五年内向其他省市铺开。可以肯定的是，转变职能，实现从"管理"到"服务"的转变，已经成为全国各级政府的共识。

目前，小微企业免征营业税和增值税已经使全国超过600万户企业受益，减税规模达200亿左右。从政策的走向来看，这一措施还将研究形成更加稳定和全面的长效机制。不少小微企业主就表示，目前月销售额2万元的减税门槛还是偏低，很多超过2万元的小微企业盈利仍然困难，却不在这一次减免税收名单之列。如何科学地制定减免条件，广泛覆盖市场上最活跃也确实面临经营困难的小微企业，又能合理控制对财政收入的冲击，这应是激励创业新体制要研究的重要课题。

《决定》还特别鼓励高校毕业生自主创业，并提出整合发展国家和省级高校毕业生就业创业基金。大学生是相对特殊的创业群体，他们刚刚从学校毕业，经验、资源、社会关系非常有限，面临更大的创业困难和经济风险。整合创业基金直接解决的就是大学生资本不足的问题，例如通过财政转移支付实现专款专用，或充分利用金融杠杆对大学生创业贷款给予审批和利息等方面的优惠。天津市2013年就推出了高校毕业生创业扶持政策，毕业生自主创业最高可以获得30万元的小额担保贷款，新公司开办3年内也不用缴纳登记、证照类行政事业性收费，并且能享受到一定程度的免税。虽然黄亦楠的创业启动资金来自她参加学校创业大赛的奖金，并没有为钱发愁，但听说天津有这样的政策，她还是很羡慕。对更多像黄亦楠一样的高校学子来说，国家明确扶持高校毕业

生自主创业为他们的人生规划提供了另一种可能。创业这条道路必然不会平坦，但越来越明确的政策激励和切实的政策优惠正在成为每一个创业者实现梦想的助推器。

第三节　保障劳动权利

大连女孩小雯2012年大学毕业，成绩十分优秀。早在2011年9月，小雯就在刚开始不久的校园招聘季中与首都航天机械公司达成就业意向。经过面试及体检，双方于10月底签订了就业意向书。2012年6月，正在拍毕业照的小雯高兴地接到公司来电，通知她7月份办理入职手续并签订一份五年期的正式劳动合同，公司随后还会为她安排统一的新员工培训。一切都进行得很顺利，但令小雯始料未及的是，上班还不到一个月，她竟然意外地被公司解聘了。在解聘通知书上，公司客气地写道："因你患有抑郁类疾病，根据你我双方签订的《普通高等院校应届毕业生接收协议》第二条第5款之规定，你不符合与公司订立劳动合同的条件，公司将你的档案退回学校。"

原来小雯在参加公司新员工培训期间表现出了一些抑郁症的症状，小雯对此也直言不讳。六七月份时，既要忙毕业论文，又对进入公司后陌生的职场环境没底，各种压力之下她确实有些抑郁。但小雯认为这并没有影响到她的工作，至少在培训期间，她的各项工作都完成得不错，并且积极地寻求心理辅导，在治疗后抑郁症状逐渐消失。2013年8月6日，在与公司协商未果后，小雯一纸诉状将首都航天机械公司告上法庭，认为对方侵犯了精神障碍患者的平等就业权。

其实，小雯的遭遇在当前的就业市场上并不罕见。抑郁症患者、乙肝病毒携带者、艾滋病毒携带者等都可能过不了求职中最后一道"体检关"。而用人单位在招聘中设置性别、户籍、学校、专业乃至身高体重等各种门槛更是屡见不鲜。因此，国务院办公厅在解决2013年高校毕业生就业困难的政策中特别提到，各地区、各有关部门要大力营造公平的就业环境，用人单位招用人员、职业中介机构从事职业中介活动时不得对求职者设置性别、民族等条件，招聘高校毕业生不得以毕业院校、年龄、户籍等作为限制性要求。正如小雯在诉状中所言，平等就业权是法律赋予每个劳动者的合法权利。

早在1995年1月1日起施行的《中华人民共和国劳动法》就规定，劳动者享有平等就业和选择职业的权利。第十二条则进一步明确，劳动者就业不因民族、种族、性别、宗教信仰不同而受歧视，第十三条还特别规定妇女享有与男子平等的就业权利。而自2008年1月1日起施行的《中华人民共和国就业促进法》则在第二十六条中直指"就业歧视"，规定用人单位招用人员、职业中介机构从事职业中介活动应当向劳动者提供平等的就业机会和公平的就业条件，不得实施就业歧视。针对与性别、户籍等自然属性或社会管理不同的病患歧视，《就业促进法》在第三十条中明确，用人单位招用人员不得以传染病病原携带者为由拒绝录用。2013年5月1日起施行的《中华人民共和国精神卫生法》则明确规定，精神障碍患者的教育、劳动、医疗以及从国家和社会获得物质帮助等方面的合法权益受法律保护。小雯的情况即属此例。

除却各种或显性或隐性的就业歧视，劳动者的平等就业权利还可能面临另一种形式的侵犯。2012年4月24日，湖北省利川市人力资源和社会保障局下属的城乡居民保险管理局面向社会公开招聘两名工作人员，吸引了20多人前来应聘。最终选出的两人都是人社局内部员工的子女，与招聘方有直接关系。这种"巧合"自然招致了社会的质疑，人们形象地称之为"萝卜招聘"，意思是招聘职位好比一个"坑"，里面早已种好了"萝卜"，所有的招聘条件都是围绕"萝卜"量身定制的，其他应聘者根本没有竞聘成功的机会。针对类似"萝卜招聘"的现象，国务院办公厅在《关于做好2013年全国普通高等学校毕业生就业工作的通知》中提出："规范国有单位招聘行为，完善公务员招考和事业单位公开招聘制度；探索建立国有单位招聘信息统一公开发布制度；加强国有企业招聘活动监管，在国有企业全面推行分级分类的公开招聘制度，切实做到信息公开、过程公开、结果公开。"这项着眼于"公开"的规定切中"萝卜招聘"背后各种人为操纵的弊端，通过行政监督和社会监督共同消除侵犯劳动者平等就业权的违法违规行为。

《决定》明确提出，规范招人用人制度，消除城乡、行业、身份、性别等一切影响平等就业的制度障碍和就业歧视。规范制度从根本上讲要有法可依，《劳动法》《就业促进法》《劳动合同法》等劳动领域的专门法都是规范招聘、用人制度的法律依据，中国还将继续加大法律保障力度，将就业领域的市场行为纳入到依法治国的框架之下。可以想见，如果没有《精神卫生法》，小雯维护自己就业权利的申诉主张也就无法落到实处。当然，仅有立法还是不够的，要切实维护劳动者的合法权利，劳动者的权利意识和法律观念还须进一步增强，要懂得运用法律来保护自己。在供需不平衡的就业市场上，劳动者相对于用人单位来说是弱势的一方，因此政府和社会有必要为弱势的劳动者提供完善的法律救助渠道，在更多像小雯一样遭到就业歧视的劳动者需要运用法律武器维护个人权利时，能够提供专业而有效的法律服务。《决定》里提及的"创新劳动关系协调机制，畅通职工表达合理诉求渠道"即是此义。

而对于各类就业歧视和不规范的招聘行为，政府作为市场的监管者也不能被动地等待被歧视者上门，而要主动作为，利用劳动保障部门、法律协会、同业协会和媒体等各方力量，探索、完善就业监察和监督体系，对违法违规行为做出相应的处罚。正如有些专家所指出的，类

似利川市人社局"萝卜招聘"之类的事件，大多数仍是通过举报或媒体曝光而非行政管理体系内部监察的方式引起公众关注，并且事后鲜见有关单位领导和组织者被问责，这暴露出目前公务员、事业单位招聘中还存在着监督力度不够、制度不健全等问题。其实，早在2009年人力资源和社会保障部、国家公务员局等部门就已经公布了《公务员录用考试违纪违规行为处理办法（试行）》，对如何处理考生的作弊行为做出了严格规定，但其中并没有明确考试组织实施方的责任。问责制度的缺失在一定程度上为人为操纵录用结果留下了空间，导致"萝卜招聘"屡有发生。这也是《**决定**》提出的影响平等就业的"制度障碍"之一，是政府在政治建设和社会建设领域要重点改革的对象。公务员、事业单位招聘录用工作人员，也需要在阳光下运行，通过建立公开透明的人事管理制度和切实有效的内外监督体系，确保每一个竞聘者站在同样的起跑线上，凭真本事在竞争中脱颖而出。

说到底，保障劳动权利就是着眼于效率与公平中的后者，通过保障公平形成高效有序的就业市场格局，从而实现就业数量与质量的同步提升。

第三章　收入：保护与调节

　　中国人过年时经常喜欢在大门上贴上年画"连年有余"。白白胖胖的娃娃脸上笑意盈盈，怀里抱着寓意多子的莲蓬和象征富裕的鲤鱼，表达出中国人对富足、充裕的物质生活的朴实愿望。老百姓的收入增加了，不再为生计发愁，才能过上体面、有尊严的生活。

　　改革开放30多年来，中国已经摆脱了贫穷落后的状态，成为世界上第二大经济体。中国人的物质生活水平已经得到了巨大的改善，基本实现了小康。在此基础上，中国政府一如既往把增加人民收入、保护公民合法财产、缩小收入差距、规范分配秩序作为首要的民生任务。正如改革开放总设计师邓小平所指出的，贫穷不是社会主义，实现共同富裕是判断改革开放成败的最终标准。"让发展成果更多更公平惠及全体人民"，这是中国政府对人民作出的郑重承诺。

第一节 规范分配秩序

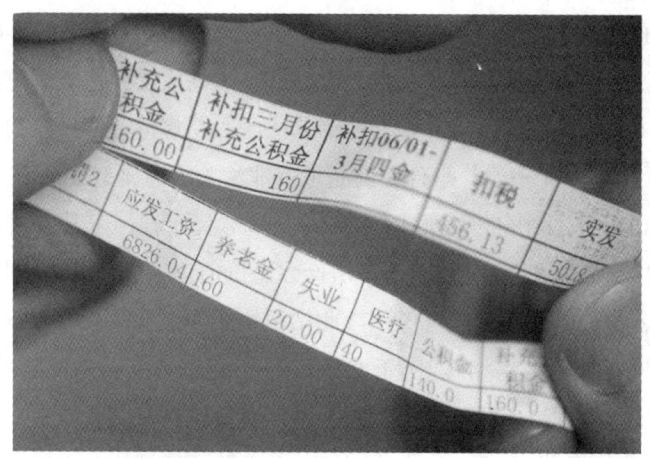

　　张燕是江苏省无锡市市直机关的一名普通科员。从2008年4月1日开始，她的工资条从原来多达十几项的各类津贴补贴变为寥寥几项：由职务和级别确定的基本工资是750元，工作性津贴2200元，生活性补贴3100元。在扣除公积金、保险和个人所得税之后，到手的实际金额在4500元左右。江苏省当年实行"阳光工资"，把公务员收入中的各类津贴补贴在清理、合并、规范后，变"暗补"为"明补"，都反映在工资里，一目了然，张燕到手的工资比调整前少了几百元。江苏省此举一是回应公务员群体收入不够透明的社会舆论，二来也为了逐渐缩小因地区和部门差异造成的公务员收入差距。

　　北京市是最早开展"阳光工资"改革的试点省市之一。早在2004年供职于海淀区某机关的杨俊就拿到了"阳光"工资单。当年7月，杨俊的工资单上收入名目少了很多，而工资总额则比上月增加了近700元。阳光工资改革的主要内容是清理整顿机关津贴、补贴、奖金并规范公务员收入，在总结试点省市改革经验的基础上，2006年7月，中国开始在全国范围内推行公务员工资制度改革，同时对中央机关和各省市津贴补贴发放进行清理规范，目标是使全国800万公务员的收入走到阳光下。

近年来，对于规范收入分配秩序，中国政府在制度层面的改革从未放松。2013年2月，国家发改委、财政部、人力资源和社会保障部联合发布《关于深化收入分配制度改革的若干意见》，提出改善收入分配秩序就必须有力保护合法收入，合理调节过高收入，有效规范隐性收入，坚决取缔非法收入。其中，取缔非法收入是规范分配秩序的重要环节。2013年的"'房姐'事件"就是取缔非法收入的典型案例。

2013年1月中旬，互联网上有人发帖称陕西省神木县农村商业银行副行长龚爱爱在北京有20多套房产，总价值近10亿元，她同时还有另一个名为"龚仙霞"的身份证。此帖很快成为公众舆论的焦点，龚爱爱也被网友称为"房姐"。由于北京市购买商品房有明确的限购规定，北京市警方根据这条线索深入调查，证实龚爱爱拥有四个户口，在北京拥有41套住房共9666.9平米。9月24日，陕西省靖边县人民法院公开审理龚爱爱伪造、买卖国家机关证件一案。由于龚爱爱此前曾担任当地商业银行副行长一职，公众对她所持有的巨额财产来源合法与否、是否利用职务之便参与经济犯罪也提出了质疑。陕西省常务副省长江泽林表示，针对"房姐"的资金来源，有关部门已着手调查，调查结果将如实向社会披露。

规范收入分配秩序需要进一步健全法律法规，加快制度建设，加强监督管理，以形成长效机制。正如《决定》所提出的，规范收入分配秩

序必须完善收入分配调控体制机制和政策体系,建立个人收入和财产信息系统,保护合法收入,清理规范隐性收入,取缔非法收入。例如保护普通劳动者的合法工资收入,就要求健全相应的工资支付保障机制,政府将把拖欠工资问题突出的领域和容易发生拖欠的行业纳入重点监控范围,完善与企业信用等级挂钩的差别化工资保证金缴纳办法,由行政系统和司法机关联动打击恶意欠薪行为,并完善劳动争议处理机制,加大劳动保障监察执法力度,以保证劳动者的合法收益。而对于党政机关各种津贴补贴和奖金等工资外收入,政府则会进一步依法清理整顿,出台规范补贴的实施意见。类似"阳光工资"的实践经验完全可以在总结完善的基础上上升为长效机制,作为规范党政机关公务员收入的常态制度。领导干部的收入管理也被纳入规范分配秩序的框架中,按照《关于领导干部报告个人有关事项的规定》,督促监督各级领导干部如实报告收入、房产、投资、配偶及子女从业等情况,并做好实际调查,对报告信息实行动态管理。

健全现代支付和收入监测体系也将成为政府的重要工作。通过薪酬支付工资化、货币化、电子化,加快现代支付结算体系建设;落实金融账户实名制,推广持卡消费,规范现金管理;完善机关和国有企事业单位发票管理和财务报销制度,全面推行公务卡支付结算制度,最终目的是把个人、企事业单位和国家机关的现金流动纳入金融监管体系之下。

在相关信息技术和网络技术的支持下,政府也将整合公安、民政、社保、住房、银行、税务、工商等相关部门的信息资源,建立健全社会信用体系和收入信息监测系统,从而真正实现透明、公开。在这方面,住房和城乡建设部已经在推动全国住房信息联网的工作。

《论语》说:"有国有家者,不患寡而患不均。"可见,中国古人早就认识到了社会分配的重要性。这种观念也为今天政府治理社会提供了最朴素的政治智慧。公正合理、公开透明是收入分配秩序的目标,在十八届三中全会对改革做出的顶层设计下,配合其他政策,采取多种手段,中国政府将积极稳妥地解决现存分配秩序的问题,朝着共同富裕的社会理想迈进。

第二节 减轻个税负担

2011年9月1日,新的个税法正式生效。白领们拿到上个月的工资后纷纷在网上晒起了工资条。张雨大学毕业已经两年,在北京一家外贸设备进出口公司从事销售工作。他先晒了7月份的工资条,其中基本工资为3850元,其他收入980元,应得工资一共是4830元;扣除掉各类保险和住房公积金,最后按2000元的个人所得税起征点算下来,共须扣税172.23元。9月6号发放的8月份工资条上,"三险一金"都不变,但由于个税起征点调到了3500元,所以这个月仅扣税14.17元,一下子减少了158.06元。对于月光族的张雨而言,这也是一笔小小的收益,张雨开玩笑说,至少可以以每个月多请女朋友吃顿饭了。

从2000元提高到3500元,这是中国的工资薪金适用个人所得税扣除标准的第三次调整。《中华人民共和国个人所得税法》于1980年颁布实施,至今已经历了6次修改,其中,2005年第3次修改时,将工资薪金上税起征点从800元提高到1600元;2007年第5次修改时,又从1600元上调至2000元。

2011年4月20日,考虑到国民收入的增加和物价水平的逐年提高,为减轻中低收入人群的负担，国务院向全国人大常委会提交了个人所得税法修正案草案，拟将工资薪金所得适用的起征点从 2000 元提高到 3000 元，相应税制结构从 9 级降到 7 级。4 月 25 日草案一审后，全国人大常委会面向社会广泛征求对个税法修正案草案的意见。由于个人所得税关系到每个公民的切身利益，公众的关注度非常高。人大常委会在短短一个多月里共收到 23.7 万多条意见，创下近年中国立法公开征求意见数量之最。结果显示，在 23.7 万多条公众意见中，约有 83% 的人认为草案里将起征点定为 3000 元还是太低。另有不少意见认为，个人所得税应该考虑不同地区经济发展水平的差异，并按家庭征收。

5 月 10 日和 20 日，全国人大分别邀请了部分专家学者和社会公众代表参加座谈，听取他们对个税法修改的意见。应邀参加座谈的社会公众代表有大学教师、在企业里从事财务工作的负责人，也有来自基层的市场销售和普通职员。王垠是山西省长治市潞安矿业集团常村煤矿的工人，来北京前做了大量准备。他不但计算自己的收支情况，也在工友中展开调查，另外还上网查阅了大量的文献资料，并收集了周围很多人的意见。在调查中王垠发现，一线工人月收入在 3000 元至 4500 元左右，目前的个人所得税税负对于他们而言有些重。他建议以 3000 元为起征点，通过降低税率来切实减轻中低收入家庭的税负，比如将 5% 和 10% 两档税率降低到 2% 和 5%。

6 月 27 日上午，草案再次提交人大常委会审议。当天的分组审议中，常委会组成人员对草案展开了热烈的讨论。有委员指出，超过 83% 的公众意见要求提高起征点，草案须对此作出有效反馈。6 月 28 日和 29 日，全国人大法律委员会两次召开会议逐条研究了常委会组成人员的审议意见，认为对个人所得税法进行修改是必要的，可以进一步降低中低收入者的税收负担，加大税收调节收入分配力度，同时建议将起征点提高至 3500 元。6 月 30 日，人大常委会通过了个税法修改的决定，将起征点提高至 3500 元，9 级超额累进的税制结构改为 7 级，并对相关的级次和税率进行了调整。

　　个人所得税不仅关乎国家的财政收入，也关乎百姓的"钱袋子"。合理征收个税既能保证公民履行纳税义务，又能切实减轻税负，实现收入增长。《决定》提出，着重保护劳动所得，努力实现劳动报酬增长和劳动生产率提高同步，提高劳动报酬在初次分配中的比重；完善以税收、社会保障、转移支付为主要手段的再分配调节机制，加大税收调节力度。对绝大多数工薪阶层劳动者的工资、薪金征收个人所得税，不仅是国家的财税体制问题，也是实际的民生问题，而民生的核心就是让普通百姓获得真正的实惠。2011年的新个税法最大的受益者就是占人口多数的中低收入群体。在个税起征点调至3500元后，纳税人负担总体减轻，工薪收入者的纳税面由之前的28%下降到约7.7%，纳税人数从大约8400万降至约2400万。仅仅是提高1500元，就使6000万人不再需要缴纳个税。

　　当然，作为调节个人收入的杠杆，目前中国的税制设计仍有许多需要完善的部分。《决定》提出，要逐步建立综合与分类相结合的个人所得税制，这是未来个人所得税制的改革方向。中国目前实行的个税是分类税制，将个人各种来源不同、性质各异的收入所得进行分类，分别扣除不同的费用，按不同的税率课税。除工资薪金外，另有劳务报酬所得、财产转让或租赁所得、股息、红利等10种。受制于当前的税收征管环境和条件，中国的个税征管机制仍以间接税为主，从源征税、代扣代缴。但随着经济高速发展，改革开放三十多年来，个人收入的来源已经呈现出多元化特点，因此个人所得税中除代扣代缴的工资收入外，对其他收入，尤其是高收入者的多元化收入征收监管的难度较大。《决定》提出的综合与分类相结合的个税制度可以更好地解决这些问题，再通过引入赡养、抚养等差别化扣除，进一步减轻工薪阶层的税收负担。

总的来说，减轻税负有利于在更大范围内、在更深层次上实现收入分配改革，保护和鼓励全社会的劳动积极性，从而增强经济社会发展的活力。

第三节　缩小收入差距

唐波是重庆市一家摩托车企业的普通职工。拿到上个月的工资单时，看着到手的工资涨了500多块钱，她特别高兴。几个月前工会在一线工人中征求意见，向公司领导层积极争取涨工资。唐波在车管油箱分厂车间工作，因刺激性气体对身体健康有影响，她和车间里其他90多个工友每个月都增发了200元补贴，加上计件工资标准上调，又增加了300多元收入。这次工资调整与以往相比，主要面向的是一线员工和低收入员工。调整的最终结果是公司高层一分不涨，中层涨3%，一线涨得最多，达到18%。

"涨工资"在中国互联网上是一个热门话题,一句"跑得过刘翔,也跑不过CPI"道出了工薪阶层的心声。与此同时,贫困山区的孩子吃不起午饭、少数高收入群体的奢侈性消费等新闻和故事又刺激着大众的眼球。不同地区、不同行业、不同人群之间的收入差距已经是不争的事实,并且还有进一步拉大的趋势。2013年1月,国家统计局公布了2003年至2012年中国居民收入的基尼系数,2012年为0.474。虽然从2008年的最高值0.491开始逐年回落,但在过去的十年,系数平均值一直高位运行,达到0.482,高于国际公认的警戒线0.40。缩小收入差距,让全体公民从改革发展中受益,防止两极分化给社会带来的不稳定因素,已经成为摆在中国政府面前的严峻课题。

中国政府把缩小收入差距的突破口定位为"调高、补低、扩中",也即调整控制高收入人群的收入基数和变动幅度,逐步提升中低收入人群特别是低收入者的收入水平和增长速度,扩大中等收入人群的比例。2013年2月,国家发改委、财政部、人力资源和社会保障部联合发布《关于深化收入分配制度改革的若干意见》,提出要逐步缩小收入分配差距,使城乡、区域和居民之间收入差距较大的问题得到有效缓解,扶贫对象大幅减少,中等收入群体持续扩大。

扩大中等收入群体,自然就要促进中低收入职工工资合理增长。《意见》督促各地建立反映劳动力市场供求关系和企业经济效益的工资决定及正常增长机制,并完善工资指导线制度,根据经济发展、物价变动等因素适时调整最低工资标准。以深圳市工资指导线制度为例,2012年,该市人力资源部门从7万多份问卷调查中经过分析,确定每月工资指导价分为三个档次:高位数25830元,同比增长1.7%;中位数3087元,同比增长 3.9%；低位数 1600 元，同比增长 12.4%；三档平均数为 3892 元，比上年同期增长 17%。可以看到，低位数和平均数增长幅度较大，这一方面与最低工资标准连年上调有关，另一方面也说明近年来基层劳动者、中低收入劳动者的权益受到更多重视。在全国层面，截至 2013 年 9 月 1 日，已有 24 个省（区、市）上调了最低工资标准。按照《意见》的规定，到 2015 年绝大多数地区的最低标准应达到当地城镇从业人员平均工资的 40% 以上。

同时，《意见》针对部分过高收入行业的国有及国有控股企业，规定要严格实行企业工资总额和工资水平双重调控政策，逐步缩小行业工资收入差距；建立企业高管人员差异化薪酬分配制度，对行政任命的国有企业高管人员薪酬水平实行限高，并使其增幅低于企业职工平均工资增幅，以此逐步缩小国有企业内部分配差距。2002 年，中国开始推行国企高管年薪制时曾规定高管年薪不得超过职工平均工资的 12 倍。不过，由于中国经济的发展和国企盈利的增长，这一数字早已被突破。所以在 2009 年，中央政府下发了《关于进一步规范中央企业负责人薪酬管理的指导意见》，对中央所属国有企业的负责人薪酬确定了五项基本原则：坚持市场调节与政府监管相结合；坚持激励与约束相统一；坚持短期激励与长期激励相兼顾；坚持负责人薪酬增长与职工工资增长相协调；坚持完善薪酬制度与规范补充保险、职务消费等相配套。财政部则在当年 2 月印发的《金融类国有及国有控股企业负责人薪酬管理办法

（征求意见稿）》中明确规定，国有金融企业负责人最高年薪为税前280万元人民币。限薪的效果可以从2012年国有金融企业公布的财报中看出来，工商银行、农业银行、中国银行和建设银行四大国有商业银行行长平均薪酬为104万，与民生、平安、光大、招商4家股份制银行行长468万元的平均薪酬相比，只是后者的1/4。

通过提高中低收入群体工资水平，限制国企高管薪酬，"调高、补低、扩中"在缩小收入差距上确实发挥了一定的作用。但0.474的基尼系数水平和社会对收入差距拉大的普遍感受也让政府认识到，缩小收入差距将是一项长期任务。《决定》提出，健全工资决定和正常增长机制，完善最低工资和工资支付保障制度，调节过高收入，增加低收入者收入，扩大中等收入者比重，努力缩小城乡、区域、行业收入分配差距，逐步形成"橄榄型"分配格局。"橄榄型"分配格局的提法就是针对中国目前收入分配格局呈金字塔型而言的，把垂直的"上面小，下面大"变为水平的"两头小，中间大"，为缩小收入差距指明了具体方向。值得注意的是，《决定》把非公有制经济也定位为社会主义市场经济的重要组成部分，从产权保护、公平竞争、财税体系上给予更多支持，将有利于提高非公有制经济尤其是民营中小企业的发展水平，而民营中小企业在解决社会就业中发挥着巨大作用，因此有助于在更大范围内提高普通劳动者的薪酬待遇。民营中小企业的进一步发展与工资指导线制度相结合，将加速企业内部工资谈判机制的建立，推动本不具备强制性的工资指导线制度发挥更大的实际功效。而对于收入普遍不高的农村居民，《决定》也规定要赋予农民更多财产权利，通过土地流转制度改革、集体经济组织市场运作、宅基地制度改革等多种手段，探索农民增加财产性收入的渠道，使农民从土地增值中获得收益。这就意味着，占人口多数的农村居民的增收问题也被纳入全会改革发展战略的整体框架中，以"补低"来缩小收入差距的思路将覆盖更大的人群范围，并且有更多改革措施的配套支撑。

"调高"方面的工作也在积极推进。2013年5月人力资源和社会保障部牵头进行的针对央企和国企高管收入的调研已经基本结束。这将为政府出台旨在规范部分收入过高的行业和央企、国企高管的降薪措施提供依据，以弥合央企、国企高管与公务员以及企业内部基层员工的收入差距。由于多数央企高管在身份上同时又是具有行政级别的官员，在退休、养老等各个方面已拥有充足的保障，因此过高地分享国有资产运行的市场红利有失社会公平。中共十八届三中全会之后，这一高收入群体的降薪将成为主旋律。而对非国有金融企业和上市公司高管的薪酬，政府则会采取不同于行政干预的市场化和法律化手段，通过完善公司治理结构，增强董事会、薪酬委员会和股东大会的监管等来抑制畸高薪酬。

中共十八届三中全会召开前由人民网发起的网络调查中，约有1/3的网友在10个民生热门关键词中选择了"收入差距"。这说明，正视收入差距拉大的现实、努力缩小收入差距，已经是民众对下一步改革的重要期待。要形成"橄榄型"分配格局，实现发展成果由全体人民共享，降低转型期改革发展的社会风险，缩小收入差距是必经之路。

第四章 社会保障：关怀与公平

"老有所终，壮有所用，幼有所长，矜寡孤独疾废者皆有所养"，这是中国古人对理想世界的描绘。今天，在中国很多地方，城镇和农村的退休老人都能按月领取养老金，劳动者和用人单位按比例共同缴纳社会保险和住房公积金，孤寡、残疾、失业等困难群体可以享受国家给予的最低生活保障等救济性福利。现代的社会保障制度为中国人展现出另一幅理想社会的图景。

社会保障是政府为公民提供的最基本的公共服务。在中国，社会保障往往被简称为"五险一金"，由养老保险、医疗保险、失业保险、工伤保险、生育保险和住房公积金构成，通过调动国家、社会和个人三方的力量共同建立起一整套关怀体系，切实解决了老百姓的后顾之忧。今后，中国的社会保障制度将兼顾效率与公平，在更高的水平上实现基本保障全覆盖、城乡保障一体化、保障结构多层次的格局。

第四章 社会保障：关怀与公平

第一节 统筹养老保险

2007年2月，原广州港港湾医院在企业改制中由广州港集团移交给广州医学院。移交中规定，2005年7月30日前退休的医院员工人事关系留在广州港集团公司，按企业退休职工管理；7月30日之后退休的员工则随医院转入广州医学院，按事业单位退休人员管理。李姨在退休前是正高级职称的医生，由于在规定时间前退休，因此只能按企业退休职工算，每月的退休工资为2000多元，企业职工养老金全国统一上调后，也才刚刚超过3000元。而李姨的同事在企业转制后按事业单位退休的，正高级职称每月却能领到5000多元的退休金，几乎比李姨多出一倍。同样在医院贡献了几十年，退休后的待遇却有这么大的差别，李姨心里很不平衡。

实际上，企业与事业单位的差别久已存在。以广州市目前的退休平均待遇来看，在政府机关里任职的最低职位——科员，退休金一般都能拿到3000多元，再往上，副科级有4000多元，正科级5000多元，副处级则能达到7000元左右。也就是说，公务员即使一直以科员身份工作到退休，退休金通常也能比普通的企业职工多出两三倍。

根据不同用工性质采取不同的退休养老金制度，这在中国称为"双轨制"，它是计划经济时代向市场经济转型期的特殊产物。1992年中国养老保险改革时规定：政府机关和事业单位退休实行由财政统一支付的

养老金制度，个人不缴纳或很少缴纳社会保险；而企业职工则实行由企业和职工本人按一定标准缴费的"缴费型"统筹制度。从1992年开始实施到今天，两种制度下的养老金形成了巨大的差异。比如，公职人员不交社保，退休后却能领到工资替代率达80%左右甚至更高的养老金；而城镇企业员工的退休金替代率只有45%。

最近几年，国家逐渐意识到了双轨制的问题，并采取积极措施进行调整，从2005年起每年都按一定幅度提高企业退休人员的养老金。2013年1月9日，国务院召开常务会议，决定从1月1日起按照10%的标准上调企业退休人员基本养老金，这是企业职工养老金连续第9年上调。此次上调之后，全国平均水平已突破1800元。而根据会议提供的数据显示，就全国平均水平而言，2012年企业退休人员每月养老金达到1721元，与2005年调整前700元的水平相比增加了一倍多。69岁的吕明昌是山东省东营市旅游服务公司的职工，2004年从单位退休，到去年底，他的养老金已经从刚退休时的不到700元涨到2528元。现在，他一个人的养老金就能维持家庭的日常开支，老伴儿的退休金完全可以存起来。

与此同时，国家也针对双轨制的另一轨有步骤地推进养老金改革。2008年2月，国务院常务会议讨论并原则通过了《事业单位工作人员养老保险制度改革试点方案》，确定在山西、上海、浙江、广东、重庆

5省市先期开展试点,与事业单位分类改革配套推进。方案的核心就是参照企业职工养老保险的管理办法,在事业单位实行社会统筹和个人账户相结合的基本养老保险制度,由单位和个人按一定的比例分别缴纳养老保险,同时建立职业年金制度作为基本养老保险之外的补充。不过,改革的推进并不顺利,五省市中只有广东率先"破冰",事业单位职工与企业职工一样按月缴纳养老保险,但退休时待遇依然按旧办法执行,改革打了一个不小的折扣。

  针对养老金实际运行中的双轨制和事业单位养老保险改革试点中遇到的重重阻力,《决定》提出,要建立更加公平可持续的社会保障制度,坚持社会统筹和个人账户相结合的基本养老保险制度,推进机关事业单位养老保险制度改革。人力资源和社会保障部副部长胡晓义在2013年7月曾公开表示,养老金双轨制"并轨"的大方向是明确的,但并不是简单地把机关事业单位退休制度"并入"企业养老保险制度,而是朝着一个共同的方向改革和推进,最终取消"双轨制"。人保部有关官员认为,在此前的改革试点中把事业单位划分成不同类别和等级,只拿其中一小类来改革,导致无法凝聚共识、形成合力。在中共十八届三中全会之后,政府将在推进事业单位分类改革的基础上,同步推进机关事业单位社会保险制度改革。由于机关事业单位现行退休养老制度已实行60多年,只有在完善的顶层设计之下循序渐进,从机构分类、人事制度、工资分配、财政保障等多方面出台配套措施,做好企业与机关事业单位各项社会保险制度的有效衔接,才能实现旧制度的平稳过渡,减少社会震荡。

  除了双轨制导致的不公平,目前中国养老保险还面临如何实现全国统筹的问题。由于养老金长期处于地区分割统筹状态,导致不同经济发展水平地区的养老保险实际缴费率相差悬殊。例如2011年广东省企业实际缴费率仅为5.9%,而甘肃省则高达24.5%,如此严重的差异违背了法定养老保险制度公平筹资的原则。而地区分割统筹还造成了养老金的结构性缺口,像广东、浙江、北京、上海等经济发达地区的养老基金结余持续增加,而其他多数中西部省份则因收不抵支只能靠财政补贴来维

持运营,如2011年广东的养老基金累计结余已逾3600亿元,而黑龙江、辽宁的年度养老金收支缺口却分别达到了183亿元和156亿元。即便是在广东省内部,因没有实现省级统收统支,不同市县之间养老金余缺并存,粤北等经济相对欠发达的市县空账也需要通过财政予以填补。

针对这一现象,《决定》明确提出,要实现基础养老金全国统筹,坚持精算平衡原则;完善社会保险关系转移接续政策。实行基础养老金全国统筹的目的是在全国各地区实现企业职工基本养老保险政策的基本统一,这一方面可以从根本上解决跨地区流动就业人员的养老保险关系转移及其权益保障问题,避免再次出现2007年底深圳80多万人退保的局面;另一方面还可以扩大调剂范围,逐步改变各地区养老保险基金不均衡的状况。但在推进全国统筹的过程中必然会面临养老基金结余较多的地区不愿意上交权力等改革阻力,对此人保部社会保障研究所所长金维刚认为,实现统筹的关键在于合理划分中央与地方对基本养老金的筹资和支付责任,明晰双方的事权与财权,共同支撑养老保险制度以及基金的平稳运行。

"让发展成果更多更公平惠及全体人民"并不是一句空话。无论是改革机关事业单位养老保险制度,还是实现养老基金全国统筹,都是着眼于建立公平可持续的社会保障制度,为不同地区、不同职业的退休老人提供同样稳定可靠的养老保障。

第二节 应对老龄难题

69岁的胡老爷子虽然已经退休了好几年,却依然保持着上班时的作息:上午八点半到,下午四点半走。不过他去的可不是工作场所,而是北京阜成门附近的新街口养老院。虽然每天从家到养老院坐公交车往返要花4个小时,但胡老爷子还是风雨无阻。新街口养老院的文化生活很丰富,有志愿者教老人们做手工、剪纸、书法甚至是唱歌,他从广播里听说后直接就过来了。胡老爷子的老伴走得很突然,家里一下子变得空荡荡的,他又舍不下家,干脆办了日托手续,每天只需要花20块钱就能吃一顿午餐,在养老院提供的床上睡个午觉。日托中心位于地下室,冬暖夏凉,凑够4个人还可以玩麻将,胡老爷子对日托中心很满意。

但黄新芸的晚年生活却是另一番景象。她退休前是大学里的副教授,离婚多年,一直一个人住,家里很少有人来。年轻时的黄新芸很要强,根本没想过老的一天。直到六年前患了一场大病,她整天面对着手术、病房和抬不起的腿,突然觉得被时间打败了。病痛和孤独让黄新芸常常想尽快结束生命。

胡老爷子和黄新芸的不同生活只是中国老龄社会的一个缩影。截至2012年底,中国大陆60周岁及以上人口达到19390万人,占总人口的14.3%,比2011年提高0.59个百分点。统计机构预计到2020年,60周岁以上人口数将达到2.43亿,2025年将突破3亿。老龄化已经成为现实的社会问题,考验着政府提供基本养老公共服务的能力。虽然近十年来,中国通过养老保险、医疗保险和最低生活保障制度等多种举措基本建立了覆盖全社会的保障体系,但在加速到来的老龄化面前,养老保障在广度、深度和力度上距离满足全社会老龄人口的正常养老需要还有很大差距。

2013年9月6日,国务院发布了《关于加快发展养老服务业的若干意见》。《意见》指出,养老服务和产品供给不足、市场发育不健全、城乡区域发展不平衡是目前养老服务业最突出的问题。要想实现到2020

年全面建成以居家为基础、社区为依托、机构为支撑,功能完善、规模适度、覆盖城乡的养老服务体系这一目标,国家需要从规划城市养老服务设施、发展居家养老服务网络、加强养老机构建设、加强农村养老服务、繁荣养老服务消费市场、积极推进医疗卫生与养老服务相结合等六个方面入手。

显然,要做的工作还很多,但现实的压力却越来越大。根据一家媒体在80后人群中进行的调查,超过半数以上的受访者由于与父母分居两地、赡养多位老人、生活工作压力较大等原因,认为居家赡养老人存在着困难。机构养老则面临着资源紧张的困境。根据民政部的统计,2012年全国各类养老服务机构共有44304个,拥有床位416.5万张,每千名老年人拥有养老床位21.5张,年末收养老年人293.6万人。对比老龄人口的数量,养老机构提供的服务资源和服务能力还存在着巨大的缺口。以北京市为例,2012年有记者调查后发现,北京数十家公办养老院床位都已满额,老人要想住进去必须排号。床位最紧张条件也最好的第一社会福利院有1100张床位,但排号等待的已达7000多人,老人要住进来至少得等10年。

由此,发动社会力量参与养老事业、大力发展社区养老成为破解养老难题的重要突破口。《北京市"十二五"时期老龄事业发展规划》提出"9064"养老服务模式,即到2020年实现90%的老年人通过社会化服务在家庭养老,6%通过政府购买服务在社区托老,4%入住养老服务机构集中养老。此前,北京已探索通过政府购买服务的方式为80周岁及以上的老年人每人每月发放100元的养老券,满足老年人在生活照料、家政服务、康复护理等方面的基本生活服务需求。利用城乡社区公益性用房、单位内部设施、居民空闲房屋等社会资源设立的养老餐桌,以及利用现有的社区服务中心、社区"星光老年之家"、社区"残疾人温馨家园"、职业康复中心等服务场所建立的社区托老所也逐步投入运行。2013年10月,北京市出台了《关于加快本市养老机构建设的实施办法》,通过土地、税费、补贴等多种手段鼓励社会资本投资建设非营利性或营利性的养老机构。市属的公办公营养老机构也可以通过招标等方式交由社会力量运营,实现投资运营主体的多元化。之前社会热议的床位数满10张且符合其他条件就可以申请开办养老机构也同时得到落实。

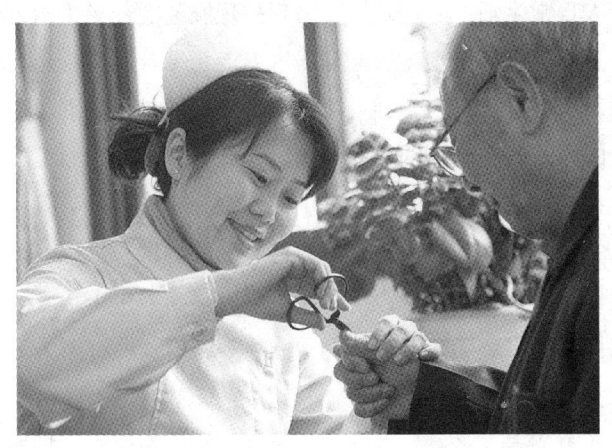

《决定》要求积极应对人口老龄化,加快建立社会养老服务体系和发展老年服务产业。未来中国应对老龄化难题的基本思路可以归纳为:政府从公共产品供给角度提供政策引导以及包括养老保险、医疗保险等在内的基本保障,调动市场和社会的力量参与养老服务事业,通过产业化途径供给市场产品,以解决目前养老服务业资本不足、资源紧张、发展滞后的现状。养老是政府义不容辞的责任,引入社会力量来办养老机构,并不是要把养老的职责和任务完全推向社会。在政府提供养老基本保障的基础上,发挥社会力量的作用,吸引其参与到养老事业中来,可以打破垄断,引入市场竞争,有利于进一步提高机构养老服务的质量。

可以预见的是，即便是调动更多资本和人力进入养老服务业，养老机构一床难求的局面短期内也难改变，建设达到一定数量规模的能够统筹好老人日常生活、心理疏导、医疗护理服务的养老机构更非朝夕之功。在这个前提下，社会化服务与居家养老相结合就成为养老政策措施的一个创新点，这既符合中国人习惯居家养老的传统心理习惯，又能够以专业化的方式解决老人的养老需求。如此一来，老人原有的社会关系网仍然存在，与儿女之间因赡养产生的摩擦和矛盾也可以大大减少，像北京等地的养老券和养老餐桌就是值得鼓励的尝试。虽然养老券在运作过程中也暴露出不少问题，包括适用范围有限、提供市场服务的商家认可度和积极性不高、无法与现金等同兑换等，但这些都不失为解决养老需求的有益尝试。

而对于方兴未艾的社区养老，很多基层社区在资本、场所、人力投入上都捉襟见肘。这就需要政府对社区养老发展的现状和问题进行实际调查，有步骤地引导和帮助基层社区解决困难，落实社区养老服务。例如北京市统一要求今后新建居住区须根据规划要求和建设标准，配套建设养老机构，并与住宅同步规划、同步建设、同步验收。对于老城区和已建成小区无养老机构或现有设施没有达到规划和建设指标要求的，要限期通过购置、置换、租赁、腾退等方式开辟养老机构。

养老是每个人都将面临的生存问题。保障每个公民的晚年生活有尊严、有安全感和幸福感，政府责无旁贷。中共十八届三中全会对养老服务业发展做出积极部署，正是为了努力应对已经到来的老龄化浪潮，以期走出"未富先老"的困境。

第三节 安居才能安心

2012年2月6日是中国传统的元宵节，春节前刚搬进新房的曾涛夫妇把父母接了过来，连同5岁的儿子，一家人热热闹闹地过大年吃元宵。他们是北京市第一批社会化公租房的住户，60多平米的两居室新房让一家人整个春节都喜气洋洋的。曾涛和妻子宋丹从结婚开始就一直住在父母家，5年前儿子出生后，父母那套两室一厅的房子显得更加拥挤了。曾涛暗暗发愁，随着儿子长大上学，一家五口的居住问题怎么解决？2009年初，曾涛夫妇两人每月的工资加起来刚够3000元，宋丹提议去申请一套两室一厅的经济适用房，但经济适用房的轮候家庭太多，很长时间都没有消息，夫妻俩只能干着急。2011年底，北京市公租房开始面向保障房轮候家庭配租，等不及的曾涛和宋丹觉得当务之急是解决住房困难，买房的事可以从长计议，便申请了一套距离地铁一号线不到800米的公租房，很快在2012年初就搬进了新家。

与曾涛同样幸运的还有广西人江山。作为在郑州工作的外地人，江山一切都是从零开始。为了压缩生活成本，他只能在环境不尽如人意的"城中村"租一间小小的屋子作为睡觉的地方。冲着公司里干净舒适的环境，江山经常加班到晚上十点才离开。那时，江山根本没想到能在郑州住上明亮宽敞的房子。2013年9月，他正式告别"城中村"的蜗居生活，搬进了郑州市面向低收入群体提供的公租房。

江山的幸运得益于"三房合一"的新政策。2013年3月郑州市提出了将廉租房、经济适用房和公租房统一并入公租房管理体系的"三房合一"草案，确认公租房保障遵循"政府主导、企业参与、市场租金、分级补贴、先补后缴、租补分离"的原则，探索"先租后售、购买自愿"的管理新途径。7月1日起，"三房合一"正式实施，郑州成为第一个正式公开宣布停建经适房的城市。根据政策实施办法，三种保障房

"并轨"为公租房后，申请条件不受户籍限制，而租金每月最高为15元/平方米，最低为5元/平方米，承租人按照规定缴纳租金，还能享受最高不超过70%的政策优惠补贴。比如一套60平方米的两室一厅，租金最高为每月630元，最低仅为210元。

公租房、经济适用房、廉租房都是中国政府在1998年实施住房制度改革后，针对商品房价格一路上涨并超出经济困难家庭承受能力的实际推出的住房保障制度。三类住房各有政策定位，分别面向不同对象。廉租房是政府以租金补贴或实物配租的方式，向符合城镇居民最低生活保障标准且住房困难的家庭提供的保障性住房，申请者一般要同时满足当地的低收入标准和人均居住面积限制等条件。经济适用房则是具有社会保障性质的商品住宅，采取由国家统一下达计划、地方政府划拨土地的方式建设，出售时按保证微利的原则确定价格。经适房由于相对市场价格比较适中，对中低收入家庭形成很大的吸引力。但购房者也需要满足相关条件提出申请，在大多数城市往往还要摇号轮候。针对暂时无力购买经济适用房又不符合廉租房条件的收入"夹心层"，2010年6月12日，住房和城乡建设部联合发改委、财政部、国土资源部等七部委发布了《关于加快发展公共租赁住房的指导意见》，规定由地方各级政府为组织实施主体，通过新建、改建、收购等多种方式筹集房源，面向城市中等偏下收入住房困难家庭、新就业职工和有稳定职业并在城市居住一定年限的外来务工人员等群体提供租赁住房。

三类保障性住房针对中低收入者的居住需求，以政府为主导，充分利用市场的力量，兼顾效率与公平，近年来切实解决了一大批城市居民的住房问题。2013年，中国在全国范围内计划新开工城镇保障性安居工程630万套，基本建成470万套。根据住房和城乡建设部公布的数据，截至11月底，已开工666万套，基本建成544万套，已超额完成年度目标任务，完成投资11200亿元。对于保障性住房尤其是经适房在实际运作中出现的隐形腐败和不公问题，郑州市率先走出"三房合一"的第一步，即逐步建立"以租为主"的住房保障体系，发挥租金的杠杆作用，促使中国人由过去"居有其屋"向"居有其所"的观念转变。

第四章 社会保障：关怀与公平

多年来，在住房保障方面，中国政府的投入力度是很大的。早在2008年12月出台的《国务院办公厅关于加快房地产市场健康发展的若干意见》中，加大保障性住房建设力度就列在第一部分。《决定》提出，要健全符合国情的住房保障和供应体系，未来中国住房供应体系总的方向是以政府为主提供基本保障、以市场为主满足多层次需求。在构建住房供应体系中政府需要重点处理好四大关系，即政府提供公共服务和市场化的关系、住房发展的经济功能和社会功能的关系、需要和可能的关系、住房保障和防止福利陷阱的关系。

由于建设完善的住房保障体系投入较大，公共财政支付能力和土地资源等条件相对有限，因此政府也考虑引入非营利机构参与保障性住房的建设和运营管理。在这种模式下，政府负责制定住房保障政策并进行监管，具体建设项目则由第三方来执行，从而既减轻了政府的压力，便于合理把握保障性住房建设的规模和节奏，又能使建设、运营、管理更加专业、透明。

针对保障性住房尤其是经济适用房在实际运行过程中出现的隐形腐败和不公平问题，在未来的保障性住房建设和管理上，政府将在准入、使用、退出等方面建立规范机制，对非法占有保障性住房的行为进行有效的治理和惩处。其实，郑州市率先迈出"三房合一"的第一步正是防止住房保障掉入福利陷阱的举措。并轨后的公租房一来没有产权，可以避免公权力在市场上寻租；二来也不设立户籍门槛，能在更大范围内体

现公平。将多种形式的保障性住房统一为公租房，还可以简化住房保障体系，便于政府监管和社会监督，有利于住房供应体系的整体设计与布局。"郑州经验"极有可能在全国推广开来。

衣食住行是每个人的基本物质生活需求，安居才能安心。江山搬进公租房后真正感到在郑州这个陌生的城市有了根。可见，完善的住房保障不仅与个人的幸福感受相连，也关系到社会的稳定与发展。

第四节 完善农村社会保障

2009年，家住山西省吕梁市柳林县郝家坡村的郭云厚老汉领到了有生以来第一笔养老金。这在习惯了"养儿防老"的农村可是件大事。一辈子都是农民的郭老汉从来没想过，在自己65岁的时候能像城里人一样每个月领钱。在他年轻那会儿，这只是"公家人"才享有的待遇。手里攥着65元现金的郭老汉脸上笑开了花。对城里人来说，65块钱还不够下一次饭馆，但对这些生活在农村的老人而言，这意味着一个月的生活有了着落。65元是郭老汉拿到手的新型农村社会养老保险金，柳林县在国家财政全额支付最低标准55元的基础上又配套补贴了10元。

65元钱解决的不仅仅是农村老人的日常生活需求，也提升了他们的幸福感。河南许昌长葛市坡胡镇孟排村的村民王喜梅就觉得，手里拿着国家给的养老金，她比以前更有尊严了。住在农村可以自己种粮喂鸡，吃住都不花钱，现在要买点其他东西完全可以用每个月60元的养老金，不用再向儿女们伸手要。带着小孙子路过村里的小卖部时，她也掏得起钱买些零食给孩子了。

一切改变都源自2009年中央政府启动的新型农村社会养老保险（以下简称"新农保"）试点。参照城镇企业职工的养老保险制度，中国在人口占大多数的农村地区也开始探索建立个人缴费、集体补助和政府补贴相结合的养老保险制度，实行社会统筹与个人账户相结合，并与家庭养老、土地保障、社会救助等其他社会保障政策配套，以保障农村居民的老年基本生活。按照当年国务院发出的《关于开展新型农村社会养老保险试点的指导意见》,年满16周岁(不含在校学生)、未参加城镇职工基本养老保险的农村居民都可以在户籍地自愿参加新农保。其中,个人缴费标准设为每年100元、200元、300元、400元、500元5个档次,参保人可以自主选择档次缴费,多缴多得;政府对符合领取条件的参保人全额支付新农保基础养老金,中央确定的基础养老金标准为每人每月55元,地方政府还可以根据实际情况提高基础养老金标准;而有条件的村集体应当对参保人缴费给予补助,补助标准由村民委员会召开村民会议民主确定。

《意见》当年的试点覆盖面为全国10%的县(市、区、镇),以后逐步扩大试点,在全国普遍实施,规划到2020年之前基本实现对农村适龄居民的全覆盖。王喜梅所在的河南省是农业大省,截至2012年9月底,全省参保人数达4680万人,有1060万名适龄老人领到了政府发放的养老金。新农保的覆盖面和实际保障力度从根本上改变了农村居民"年轻时靠土地,老了靠儿女"的被动状态,消除了老人们经常会有的"再过几年干不动了怎么办"的忧虑。

不过,新农保在执行中面临一个最大的问题是年轻人参保率不高。相关学者研究后指出,除却农民参保意识不强,造成这一问题的主要原因是新农保目前的回报仍不能与企业职工养老保险和城镇居民养老保险相提并论,尤其与企业职工养老保险的差距更为显著。在中国现行的养老保险体系下，新农保是三个险种里最薄弱的一环，城乡居民之间在养老保险制度设计上还存在着一定的差距。新农保的本意是从社会保障制度上打破城乡二元结构，但如何从实现全覆盖到与其他险种无缝对接再到养老金实质公平就成了下一步必须解决的问题。

2010年10月28日，全国人大常委会第十七次会议审议通过《中华人民共和国社会保险法》，其中第二十二条规定：省、自治区、直辖市人民政府根据实际情况，可以将城镇居民社会养老保险和新型农村社会养老保险合并实施。《社会保险法》从2011年7月1日起生效，当年安徽省即宣布将新农保与城居保统一为城乡居民社会养老保险制度。一年之后，河北省也将两种社会养老保险制度合并实施，并轨后城乡居民参保缴费标准一致、养老待遇一致，个人每月缴费从100元到1000元不等的10个档次中自主选择。

地方政府的实践为在全国范围内统一推进城乡居民养老保险并轨提供了现实基础。2013年1月，人力资源和社会保障部表示，将制定实施城乡养老保险制度衔接政策，在新农保、城居保提前8年实现制度全覆盖的基础上，2013年年内推进合并实施城乡居民社会养老保险制度，涉及人数约4.8亿。《决定》明确提出整合城乡居民基本养老保险制度、基本医疗保险制度，推进城乡最低生活保障制度统筹发展。这一决定一方面是通过统筹城乡一体化发展，缩小城乡两种养老保险制度的差距，提高保障力度；另一方面也是为了简化目前的社会保险制度体系，与逐步统一企业职工养老保险和机关事业单位养老保险相呼应。

根据人保部的统计，2013年前三季度，城乡居民社会养老保险的参保人数已经达到49030万，接近全国总人口的1/4。居民养老保险已经成为覆盖人群最多的基本社会保障制度。要在全国范围内推动实施城乡居民养老保险，既要保证基础养老金在参保条件、缴费标准、待遇标准上全国统一、城乡统一，又要允许根据各地区的经济发展水平、财政收入水平、新农村建设水平以及参保人的个人意愿和缴费能力实现多层次、差异化的保障格局，从而通过两保并轨提高农村居民的养老保障力度，形成参保激励。唯有如此，才能形成具备相当水平又保证公平的城乡居民养老保险全覆盖。

第五章　医疗卫生：根基与安全

　　新中国成立60多年来，中国的医疗卫生事业发生了翻天覆地的变化。国民的人均预期寿命从1949年的35岁提高到2011年的76岁。2006年新医疗体制改革以来，覆盖城乡居民的医疗保险体系已经建立，这是医疗卫生领域取得的巨大成就。但近些年来，普通人"看病难"、"看病贵"的感受仍然存在。医疗卫生资源作为公共服务离满足全民的健康需求还有一定的差距，医疗保障体系在覆盖广度、统筹力度和保障水平上需要进一步加强，民间对放开医疗卫生事业的市场准入和改革现行生育政策的呼声也越来越高。

　　生命是个体最基本的权利，医疗卫生事业的发展与国民健康水平的提高是社会持续进步的根基。中国的医疗卫生体制改革仍须加快推进速度，为中国普通百姓的健康和安全护航。

第一节 建设全民医保

"全民医保"这个概念正式与公众见面是在2009年4月颁布的《中共中央国务院关于深化医药卫生体制改革的意见》中。全民医保,其实就是要在中国建立健全完整的医疗保险体系,使所有人患病后都能从政府主导建立的医疗保险制度中获取帮助。目前中国主要存在的基本医疗保险制度有三种,分别是城镇职工基本医疗保险、城镇居民基本医疗保险和新型农村合作医疗制度(简称"新农合")。

新农合使9亿农民受益

湖北省秭归县九畹溪镇周坪村大病刚愈的谭光英逢人便夸新农合的好处:"没想到年初交的几十元钱,现在成了我们全家的救命钱。"原来,2012年2月,谭光英被查出患有风湿性心脏病,必须马上手术治疗,否则有生命危险。在完成心脏瓣膜置换手术出院结算时,9万多元的医药费用由合作医疗补偿5万元,谭光英仅需支付4万多元。

2002年10月,国务院在《关于进一步加强农村卫生工作的决定》中明确指出:要逐步建立以大病统筹为主的新型农村合作医疗制度。这项制度主要由政府组织和引导,农民自愿参加。原卫生部农村卫生管理司司长杨青于2012年9月在接受中国政府网专访时表示,到2008年,新型农村合作医疗制度已经基本覆盖农村居民,2012年政策范围内住院

报销比例达到 75% 左右，最高支付限额不低于全国农民人均纯收入的 8 倍，且不低于 6 万块钱；而且随着门诊统筹全面开展，门诊看病也可以由医保报销部分额度。在大病问题上，许多农民个人支付能力不足，国家卫生和计划生育委员会（以下简称"卫计委"）和医疗改革办公室由此进一步以省为单位开展了 20 种重大疾病保障工作，比如儿童先天性心脏病、儿童白血病、尿毒症（中末期肾病）、脑卒中、冠心病等。安徽太湖县晋熙镇观音村农民小贾因患再生障碍性贫血，于 2012 年 3 月至 9 月住院，医药费用累计 68.03 万元，新农合补偿了其中的 48.80 万元。

从数字中可以更直接地认识这项适合于中国国情的新型农村医疗保障制度。2003 年新农合刚起步的时候只有 7000 多万农民参加，到 2008 年，全国 91.5% 的农民加入了这个制度，基本做到了全覆盖。根据相关统计，截至 2013 年 6 月底，新农合的参保人数为 8.02 亿人，参合率达到 99%，毫无疑问，这在全世界范围内也是最大的医疗保障体系。新农合由个人、集体和政府多方筹资，人均筹资标准随中国国力增强而逐渐上涨，2012 年新农合人均筹资标准达到 308.5 元，2013 年将提高到 340 元，其中各级政府补助增加到人均 280 元。预计到 2015 年，仅政府补助每人每年就将达到 360 元。随着筹资水平的不断提高，门诊和住院的报销水平也会水涨船高，农民们享受到的实际优惠将越来越多。

大病保险避免"因病致贫"

家住安徽省安庆市迎江区新洲乡天然村的方文报患有糖尿病多年，一直注射"诺和灵"针剂，每支针剂的价格是 55 元，大病统筹支付 60%，自己只需掏 22 元。每支便宜 33 元钱不是大数目，但是方文报需要常年用药，前后算下来就不是一笔小数目。同样受益的还有江苏南京江宁区贾连英一家，她在 2011 年 11 月不幸患上肺癌，两年里大病统筹报销共计 22.13 万元，全家因此避免了因病致贫。

2012 年，国家发改委等六部门颁发的《关于开展城乡居民大病保险工作的指导意见》要求推进城乡居民大病保险试点等工作。《决定》更明确地提出要加快健全重特大疾病医疗保险和救助制度。大病保险和救助制度的进一步完善同样也是公众的期待，是医改未来的工作重心之一。自 2012 年大病统筹和大病保障全面推开以来，大病患者住院费用实际报销比例已不低于 70%。截至 2013 年 10 月，已有 23 个省（区、市）出台大病保险实施方案，确定的试点城市有 120 个。2013 年 11 月，国家发改委、卫计委、财政部等六部委发布指导意见，针对城镇居民医保、新农合参保 (合) 人大病负担重的情况，将引入市场机制建立大病保险制度，避免因病致贫、因病返贫。大病保险的保障对象是城镇居民医保、新农合的参保人，所需资金从城镇居民医保基金、新农合基金中划出，不再额外增加个人缴费负担。2013 年起，农村医疗保障工作重点也已经开始向大病转移，重大疾病的实际报销比例提高到 70%。对于符合条件的贫困救助对象，民政部以医疗救助基金的形式再给予 20% 补偿，使得两者相加的报销比例不低于 90%。

医保异地结算符合民意

张桂芝原为吉林省长春市退休职工，从 1997 年开始在海南省海口市定居。由于疾病缠身，每月就医费用不菲，张桂芝习惯每次攒够 5000 元医疗费用账单后就寄回单位报销，等待约一个月后报销金额才能到账。2010 年海南开展医保异地结算后，她赶紧申办了异地就医卡。2011 年 3 月 26 日，她拿着卡不用交付押金就住进了海口市的定点医院。

中国过去长期实行医疗保障属地管理，异地医疗机构不受参保人所属医保统筹地区的政策约束和具体管理，所以甲地的患者在乙地看病无

法在乙地进行医保结算。随着中国经济发展，各个城市间人口流动性加大，异地医保结算的需求越来越强烈。2009年《关于深化医药卫生体制改革的意见》颁布后，国家紧接着推出了《医药卫生体制改革近期重点实施方案（2009—2011）》，加速推进建立居民最关心的异地就医结算机制。张桂芝就是这一政策的受益人。

到2013年8月，全国86%的职工和83%的城镇居民医保实现了市级统筹，4个直辖市和海南省、西藏自治区实现了省级统筹，新农合主要以县级统筹为主。也就是说，中国三项基本医保制度——城镇职工医保、城镇居民医保、新型农村合作医疗都已经基本实现了统筹区域范围内的就医即时结算。同时，各省份通过建立省级结算平台，也在积极推进省内异地就医即时结算。其中，新农合90%的县（市、区），以及职工和城镇居民医保在8个省（区、市）已经实现了省域内的异地就医即时结算。在跨省异地就医结算方面，各地正在通过多种方式开展探索。比如两个统筹地区签订协议，按照协议办法进行结算，海南、上海等省市就是采用的这种方法，方便了张桂芝们的生活。新农合则积极建设国家级信息平台，目前已联通北京、内蒙古、吉林等9个省级平台和29所大型医疗机构，为跨省即时结算打下了基础。

卫计委在2013年7月颁布的《深化医药卫生体制改革2013年主要工作安排》中也强调要大力推进异地就医结算，逐步推开省内异地就医直接结算，选择在部分省份试点探索建立跨省异地就医即时结算机制。当然，要在地区差异巨大的城市间实行医保结算联网，仍是一个比较大的挑战。海南的经验值得借鉴。

免费医疗的成功案例

在全面推行全民医保的进程中，还有一个令人欣喜的试验——神木县的"全民免费医疗"。神木县位于陕西省北部，2009年3月1日起县政府开始实行"全民免费医疗"，神木县的40万百姓开始享受住院看病每人每年最多可报销30万元的福利。凡是拥有神木户籍的城乡居民在定点医疗机构进行医疗，都将成为制度的受惠者。免费医疗的思路很明确：用最大认同、最可操作的方式推进医改，让人人享有统一的医疗服务和公平的社会福利，给罹患重病的病人"重生的机会"。据神木县卫生局统计数据显示，2012年全县免费医疗支出2.49亿元，报销住院医药费为2亿元，县境内的人均报销比例达84.63%，住院患者共计46084人，仅农村居民就占93.39%。这些数据可以充分证明免费医疗在神木的尝试是成功的，普通百姓成为免费医疗真正的受益者。虽然神木模式是个别案例，但其大胆的尝试对新医改的进一步推行和完善提供了有益的经验，神木模式的延续值得期待。

第二节 完善医疗服务体系

　　在湖南新邵县坪上镇医院住院的农民钟大娘说，自从卫生院条件改善后，她再也没有跑过县城和市区看病。在人们的传统观念里，农村的卫生院是陈旧简陋的，但坪上镇中心卫生院各种临床科室一应俱全，拥有500毫安X光机、进口彩色B超机、微量元素检测、中心供氧等优质设备，一扫人们对农村基层医疗机构的陈旧印象。

　　医疗卫生服务体系是一个庞大系统。截至2013年7月底，全国医疗卫生机构数达96.1万个，其中：医院2.4万个，基层医疗卫生机构92.2万个，专业公共卫生机构1.2万个，其他机构0.2万个。基层医疗卫生机构中，社区卫生服务中心（站）3.4万个，乡镇卫生院3.7万个，村卫生室65.6万个，诊所（医务室）18.3万个。在这一庞大体系中，占有数量最多的基层医疗卫生机构恰是其中最薄弱的环节，因此健全和完善基层医疗卫生服务一直都是医疗改革的工作重点。从2006年新医改开始，大量的人力、物力、资金投向基层，使基层医疗卫生机构发生巨大变化。

虽然基层医疗改革的成果有目共睹,但仍有许多需要完善和改进的地方。比如硬件越来越完备的同时,大多数基层医疗机构却普遍缺乏医疗人才。大量优质医疗资源集中在大医院,基层的社区医院的医疗资源相对缺乏,所以,大医院依然人满为患,社区医院却人丁稀少。因此,《决定》强调要深化基层医疗卫生机构综合改革,健全网络化城乡基层医疗卫生服务运行机制。同时,对下一步的改革重点也提出了明确的思路:"完善合理分级诊疗模式,建立社区医生和居民契约服务关系。充分利用信息化手段,促进优质医疗资源纵向流动。加强区域公共卫生服务资源整合。"

所谓分级诊疗模式,是指通过合理分配大医院与社区医院的医疗资源,做到小病不出社区,大病由社区医院转诊到大医院、治疗后再回社区医院康复的科学诊疗模式。只有社区医院与大医院权责明确,才能引导患者进行合理分流。例如上海市浦南医院和周边的 6 家社区卫生服务中心结成"便民联合体",并开设"家庭病床直通医院病房"的绿色通道,与社区卫生服务中心形成互补。"双向转诊"、"绿色通道"缓解了社区卫生服务中心在人员、设备、医疗技术等方面的不足。这正是分级诊疗模式的具体实践。

社区医生与居民建立契约服务关系则是指社区医生与居民签订健康管理和服务合同,双方合力管理居民的健康。从 2007 年开始,北京、上海、广州等发达城市已经陆续开始有家庭医生。北京市已组建家庭医生式服务团队 3000 余个，累计签约 361 万户居民，759 万余人。其中，65 岁以上老年人和四种慢性病患者等重点人群签约率达 70% 以上。

"中国要逐步建立可共享的电子病历与健康档案基础数据资源库。"卫计委统计信息中心副主任王才说，"卫生信息化是落实医改任务、提高医疗卫生服务质量和效率、降低医药费用、促进实现人人享有基本医疗卫生服务的重要支撑。"厦门是中国目前唯一一个成功地在城市范围内实现居民电子健康档案和相关卫生信息资源共享的城市。厦门以社会保障卡作为识别标准，为居民建设健康档案。居民用社保卡通过网络、手机、互动电视就可以预约挂号或查阅就诊结果。从出生起居民所有的健康信息、就诊病例、检查结果都会录入数据库。各个医疗机构基本实现了电子医疗记录的共享和互调，由"一院一病历"转变为"全市一卡通"。医疗电子信息化管理手段的使用，不仅省去居民到医院就诊的繁琐环节，同时也有效地解决了"挂号难"的问题。

湖北秭归县是农村信息化建设的一个典型案例。该县已经实现了直达村卫生室，覆盖省、市、县、乡、村五级定点医疗机构共计 280 个点的新农合信息化；并全面建立了居民电子健康档案，实现了病历和处方电子化，建立了涵盖基本药物制度管理、公共卫生服务、医疗服务监管、综合卫生管理、新农合制度等五大业务系统的卫生信息区域管理平台。

"中国医改的目标和总体战略是值得效仿的。中国在为全民提供平价且公平的基本医疗服务方面已经取得了巨大的成就。这不仅将影响中国的未来,也将影响全球的医疗模式。"英国权威医学杂志《柳叶刀》如此评论。

第三节 鼓励社会办医

2012年6月,历经十余年的筹建,位于北京昌平区中关村生命科学园区的北大国际医院封顶,并将于2014年试营业。与普通公立医院不同,北大国际医院是由企业出资兴办,归属于北大医疗集团,方正集团和北京大学分别拥有70%和30%的股权。这家筹备了多年的大型非营利性医疗机构总投资规模超过45亿元,集结36个医疗中心、49个学科、1800张病床,刷新了亚洲最大单体医疗建筑的纪录。作为北京市社会办医试点,北大国际医院将被纳入医保范围,市民在北大国际医院将享受和公立医院毫无差别的医疗报销,这一不同于众多民营医院的优势将吸引更多普通市民前来就医。未来五年,国家开发银行还将为北大医疗集团提供100亿元合作资金,支持其参与公立医院改革,发展医疗卫生产业。

2006年,中国新医改开始,经过三年酝酿,国务院于2009年公布了《关于深化医药卫生体制改革的意见》以及《深化医药卫生体制改革实施方案(2009—2011)》两个重要文件,指出,"鼓励和引导社会资本发展医疗卫生事业。积极促进非公立医疗卫生机构发展,形成投资主体多元化、投资方式多样化的办医体制"。2010年底,国务院再次发布《关于进一步鼓励和引导社会资本举办医疗机构的意见》,鼓励社会资本办医。同年的"十二五"医改规划中更是明确,到2015年非公立医疗机构床位数和服务量达到总量的20%左右。随着新医改的推进,各界对社会资本办医的认识也趋向一致。2012年,北京市政府首次发布针对社会资本办医的鼓励政策。这一新政被概括称为"京18条"。"京18条"显示,今后北京市将允许社会资本在京举办各级各类医疗机构,新建医院将优先安排社会资本举办，对政府办医与社会办医的政策将"一碗水端平"。

实践证明，社会办医有利于增加医疗卫生资源，扩大服务供给，提高医疗服务效率和质量。以另一个社会办医的典型——嫣然天使儿童医院为例。2011年12月23日，嫣然天使儿童医院作为一家民办非营利医院诞生。"没有刺鼻的来苏水味儿，在同一屋檐下有50张多功能病床，有能同时进行手术的4间现代化层流手术室和120多名医护人员。"嫣然天使儿童医院的常务院长刘燕群对医院进行了这样的描述。北京市卫生局的负责人认为，嫣然天使儿童医院"为慈善捐助办医做了有益的探索，同时，还可为社区的儿童提供良好的医疗服务和保健服务"。

《决定》对社会办医又进行了更完整的表述，即，鼓励社会办医，优先支持举办非营利性医疗机构。社会资金可直接投向资源稀缺及满足多元需求服务领域，多种形式参与公立医院改制重组。允许医师多点执业，允许民办医疗机构纳入医保定点范围。

国务院医改办主任孙志刚对《决定》中鼓励社会办医的改革导向做了三方面的解读：

一是优先支持举办非营利性医疗机构。对社会资本举办非营利医疗机构给予倾斜支持。特别要鼓励社会力量兴办慈善医疗机构，或向医疗救助、医疗机构等提供慈善捐赠。嫣然天使儿童医院即属于此类鼓励兴办的范围。

二是社会资金可直接投向资源稀缺及满足多元需求服务领域，并鼓励非公立医疗机构向高水平、规模化的大型医疗集团发展，拓展新兴健康服务业，如医疗康复、老年护理、临终关怀、健康咨询、美容整形、健身养生等。北京的玛丽妇婴医院、松堂临终关怀医院，佛山市南海区中村老干所医务室都是民营医疗机构中开展多元服务、诚信评级良好的范例。

三是允许社会力量以多种形式参与公立医院改制重组，在确保国有资产不流失的前提下，支持社会资本采取合作、兼并、收购等多种形式，参与包括国有企业所办医院在内的部分公立医院改制重组，增强

公立医院服务活力。社会资本参与公立医院改制,丰富了公立医院改革的形式,从某种意义上说也促进了公立医院体制改革的推进。公立医院是中国医疗服务体系的主体,在"保基本"中发挥着支柱作用,是新医改中民众关注的焦点之一。伴随公立医院体制改革进入深水区,改革面临的难度也越来越大了。而社会力量、民营资本的注入则能充分发挥各类市场主体和社会组织的作用,通过托管、参股等多种形式,参与公立医疗机构管理,形成医疗卫生服务多方参与机制,从而激发公立医院活力,加速改革进程。例如2011年北京市门头沟区政府将辖区内的京煤医院交由北京凤凰联合医院管理股份有限公司进行托管,当年度京煤医院的年收入就比上一年上涨了20%。

《决定》中允许医生多点执业同样是与鼓励社会办医有关的一个政策亮点。青岛市卫生局曾于2012年出台了《青岛市医师多点执业试点实施方案》,在该实施方案中给出了"医师多地点执业"的界定,即依法取得临床、口腔、中医类别医师资格的医师,经原注册的医疗机构同意,到相应卫生行政部门注册后,在2—3个医疗机构从事执业活动的行为。医生多点执业能够促进优质医疗资源纵向流动,大医院的医生可以流动到下一级的医疗机构坐诊,满足患者多层次的服务需求,方便患者就近得到优质医生的服务。当然,允许医师多点执业真正实施起来也依然存在管理、权职所属等方面的困难,比如出现医疗事故如何处理、谁来负责等,所以下一步政策仍须细化和规范,医师才会更愿意参与进来。

《决定》不但肯定了市场的地位,还进一步使之从"基础性作用"提升到"决定性作用"。在医疗卫生领域,随着改革的深入,触及的深层次矛盾和问题越来越多,鼓励社会力量办医,打破垄断,放开竞争,必将加速医疗体制改革的进程。

第四节 调整生育政策

从事行政工作的何慧是中国实行计划生育政策以后最早的一批独生子女,因为想给女儿再生一个做伴,她和丈夫期待"单独"政策放开已有数年之久。何慧说，小时候自己就很羡慕小伙伴家里有哥哥姐姐，希望能为女儿弥补自己童年的遗憾。今年36岁的妈妈樊适则说："现在生活压力都太大，养孩子的成本很高，奶粉、医疗、入托、择校等各方面的费用都在涨。不过，有了这样一个政策，在生第二个孩子的问题上就有了选择权。"故事中的两位妈妈关注的都是中国当前一个重要的生育话题："单独二孩"的放开。

《决定》提出，坚持计划生育的基本国策，启动实施一方是独生子女的夫妇可生育两个孩子的政策，逐步调整完善生育政策，促进人口长期均衡发展。这一政策被简称为"单独二孩"。这项新政策适用于一方是独生子女的夫妇可生育两个孩子，但首胎为双胞胎的家庭则不在政策范围内。通俗来说，计划生育政策管的是孩子数量，而不是胎次。

虽然"单独二孩"放开是计划生育政策的一次重大调整完善，但调整生育政策不等于放松计划生育工作。中国人口众多的基本国情没有根本改变，中国人口数量依然占据世界第一位，人口对经济、社会、资源、环境的压力也将长期存在，计划生育仍是中国的基本国策。实际上，计划生育政策从来不是一成不变的，一直在实践中进行着调整和完善。早在1985年，山西翼城就成为国家特批的第一个二胎试点地区，在农村试行二胎生育，此后又有多个县市进行了二胎试点；2011年，随着河南省推出双独家庭允许生育二胎的政策，全国所有省份都实现了夫妻双方均为独生子女可生育两个孩子的政策。至此，"单独二孩"的问题也越来越受到民众关注。

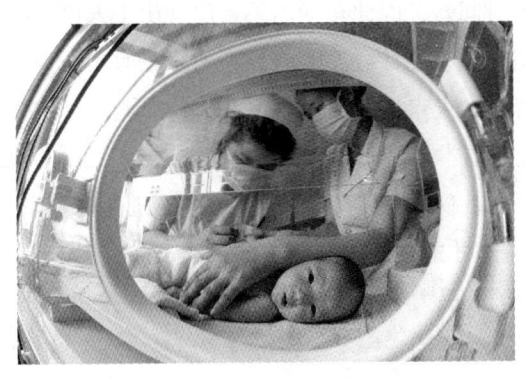

进入21世纪以来，中国人口形势发生了很大的变化。虽然人口众多仍然是中国的基本国情，但人口结构性问题已日益成为影响经济社会发展的重要因素。国家卫计委副主任王培安把这一形势概括为四点，即低生育水平稳中趋降，人口结构性问题日益突出，家庭规模持续缩减，城乡居民生育意愿发生了很大变化。自2008年起，国家卫计委就启动调整完善生育政策的准备工作，组织开展了深入的调研论证，包括"十一五"人口发展规划终期评估，"千村生育率调查"，"150个县独生子女婚育状况调查"，全国范围内0—9岁低龄人口基础信息核查等，并利用教育、公安、统计等相关部门的数据开展比对和校验，由此对全国人口总量和结构、生育现状及人口变动趋势有了比较客观、准确的判断和估计。在反复论证的基础上，2013年中共十八届三中全会启动实施了"单独二孩"政策。这项政策既是中国人口和生育政策适应经济社会发展形势所作出的适时调整，也是应对人口红利下降、劳动力短缺等问题的积极举措。

启动实施"单独二孩"政策，全国不设统一的时间表，由各省（区、市）根据实际情况确定具体时间。2013年11月19日舟山市经浙江省政府批准，率先实施"舟山海岛特批政策"——双方或一方为舟山户籍且有一方为独生子女、双方合计已生育一个子女的夫妻增列为计划生育特殊情况生育审批范围。

"单独二孩"放开后，会不会使人口激增？首先从全国来看，符合"单独二孩"条件的夫妇总量不是太大，大约有2000万，而各地启动实施政策又会有时间差，因此短期内不会出现出生人口大幅增长的问题。其次，正如国家发改委社会发展研究所所长杨宜勇所说，"新政一旦实施，每年几百万的人口增长对生育率和人口结构的影响微乎其微"。逐步放开生育政策的本意是满足多生孩子人群的生育愿望，保障这部分人的生育权。而且，政策也是有梯度的，现在仅是部分放开二孩生育，估计到2030年左右才能全面放开二胎。再次，生育意愿也未必会转化为生育行为。中国人民大学社会与人口学院院长翟振武牵头组织的一项调查显示，在近万人的调查样本中，符合"单独二孩"政策的夫妇中只有一半愿意生育第二个孩子。而 2012 年上海市人口部门进行的抽样调查显示，上海符合"双独"政策的家庭实际生育二孩的情况并不多，上海户籍 80 后家庭的平均生育意愿为 1.2 个孩子。上世纪 80 年代开始试点"二胎方案"的山西翼城、甘肃酒泉、河北承德、湖北恩施等地的农村地区到现在的平均生育意愿也全部低于 1.6 个孩子。

中国是人口大国，想要真正解决"怎么生"、"不敢生"、"生不起"的问题，仅仅放开生育数量还是不够的，更需要从错峰生育、完善优质教育和医疗资源的配置等多方面着手，继续沿着生育政策调整的良性道路发展下去。

第六章　社会治理：创新与和谐

　　中国远古时期，洪水泛滥，百姓愁苦不堪。鲧负责治理洪水，他从天上偷来"息壤"，试图堵住洪水，却没能成功。鲧的儿子禹改"堵"为"疏"，通过治理河道，把洪水导入大海，解决了水患。这就是中国有名的"大禹治水"的传说。中国共产党第十八届三中全会首次使用"社会治理"代替原来的"社会管理"，一字之差，体现的也许正是类似的执政理念。

　　社会的本质是人与人的相互关系，一个在安全稳定的政治环境和公民有序互动中形成的和谐社会，作为有机体能够实现自我调节，释放出最大的活力和创造力，为政治、经济、文化、生态等其他领域的建设营造良好的环境，从而维护国家的稳定，推动社会的进步与发展。中国政府在改革发展中必须处理好与社会的关系，充分尊重社会的自主性、适应性，把社会能够做好的交给社会，不断创新治理方式，激发社会的活力，引导公民共同参与社会治理，推动公民精神成长，确保社会既充满活力又和谐有序。

第一节　改进治理方式

上海市徐汇区凌云街道梅陇三村是个老小区，38栋老式公房里住着6500多人。人一多，社区的环境卫生就令人担忧，几年前，小区随处可见乱扔的塑料袋和饮料罐。现在，垃圾和废弃物变成了彩色的环保椅和手提袋，洁净的小区显得宁静温馨。一切改变都要归功于方翠英等10位已经退休的家庭主妇，她们自发开展"绿主妇，我当家"的环保自治行动，引导大家改变了随手乱扔垃圾的习惯。由于小区道路狭窄，一到晚上和周末，小区常常被私家车挤得水泄不通，假如发生火灾，消防车根本开不进来，由此形成巨大的安全隐患。"绿主妇，我当家"行动小组便向社区党总支和街道居委会提出了侧石翻修和道路拓宽的建议。经过翻修，小区交通环境大为改善。如今，"绿主妇"小组已经吸纳了200多名积极分子，近300户家庭成为其热心参与者，形成了梅陇三村独特的社区居民自治模式。

自从中国共产党第十六届四中全会提出构建社会主义和谐社会的目标后，中国的基层社区建设和居民自治便走上了发展的快车道。其实，对更多上了年纪的中国人来说，"居委会"是他们更为熟悉的概念。早在1989年，全国人大就审议通过了《中华人民共和国居民委员会组织法》，确定居民委员会是居民自我管理、自我教育、自我服务、自我监督的基层群众性自治组织。居委会在办理辖区居民的公共事务和公共事业、维护居民的合法权益等多方面都发挥了重要作用。"有困难，找居委会"是当时人们遇到生活中各种问题时的第一反应。

但是，上世纪八九十年代中国很多地方的居住区都是与工作单位联系在一起的，随着商品住宅的兴建和人口流动性增强，原有的居委会模式在管理效率和质量上逐渐落后于时代的需要。在这种背景下，政府提出了顺应时代发展的"社区建设"概念。2005年，民政部发布了《关于在全国推进城市社区建设的意见》，把城市社区定位为经过社区体制改革后做出了规模调整的居民委员会辖区，提出社区建设要适应城市化、现代化的要求，建立起以地域性为特征、以认同感为纽带的新型社区,构建新的社区组织体系。新的社区居委会为探索社区居民自治提供了更宽松的环境。一大批接受过培训的专职社区工作者以更加专业的服务提升了社区建设的水平。逢年过节,社区举办的居民联欢会、亲子交流活动和上门慰问空巢老人等服务在很多城市都很常见,社区越来越成为充满人情味的大家庭。

2010年11月,国务院办公厅发布了《关于加强和改进城市社区居民委员会建设工作的意见》,在社区文化建设已经发展到相当程度的基础上,突出强调社区居民自治的重要性,提出社区居委会应组织居民有序参与涉及切身利益的公共政策听证活动,开展自治活动和有关监督活动。类似"绿主妇,我当家"行动小组就不再是旧有的居民联谊组织,而主动承担起了调动居民自我管理、监督社区建设的角色。武汉市武昌区中南路街静安社区现在每个月都会召开四五次恳谈听证会,小到修缮楼道单元门,大到小区车辆管理、安装大门门禁等事务,社区都会邀请多方代表前往议事恳谈室举行听证会。2012年8月1日,居委会针对小区门禁、拦车系统年久失修导致进出人员杂乱的人财物安全问题,特意申请专项资金改造大门门禁和拦车系统,规范车辆管理。由于系统改造后居民、车辆都要买卡刷卡通行,一定程度上增加了不便,修还是不修得居民说了算,社区居委会就此组织了恳谈会。最后,在绝大多数人都同意的情况下,社区才启动了改造工程。

在总结社区建设和居民自治实践经验的基础上,《决定》提出"创新社会治理体制",首要就是"改进社会治理方式",由政府发挥主导作用,鼓励和支持社会各方参与,实现政府治理和社会自我调节、居民自治良性互动。从"社会管理"到首次提出"社会治理",反映出中国共产党和中国政府在执政理念上的变化。传统的"管理"提法着眼于政府和国家对社会公共事务直接管理,带有一定的强制性,主要运用行政手段;"治理"则在国家和政府之外还强调社会力量,包括社会组织、公民参与等,实现手段也更加多元,法律、道德和制度建设都是行之有效的途径。改进社会治理方式,就是改变原来那种自上而下的单向管理模式,在多种参与社会治理的力量主体之间形成协同互动。

中国社会科学院马克思主义研究学部主任程恩富认为,"社会治理"的提法与改革整体布局提出的"推进国家治理体系和治理能力现代化"是统一的。"治"的作用在于行使职能、提高效率,而"理"的目的在于理顺关系、明确责任。社会治理的方向就是以"治"为本,以"理"为主,打破政府无微不至"管"社会的思维惯性,强调政府在社会领域中发挥主导和协调作用,引导社会各界和多方力量带着各自的责任定位参与到共同关心的公共事务中来。政府该放则放,放而有度,放而不松;社会自我调理,理而有序,理而不乱。以未来的社区建设为例,街道办作为地方政府的行政派出机关,在社区建设中主要发挥把握方向、

落实政策、统筹协调等作用；社区建设工作的具体执行则由各社区居委会根据实际情况做出安排，在这个过程中可以充分调动社区居民自治的积极性，并且理顺社区内部、本社区与其他社区之间、社区与街道办和派出所等其他基层国家机构之间的各种关系。

《决定》还提出，改进社会治理方式，要坚持源头治理，标本兼治、重在治本，以网格化管理、社会化服务为方向，健全基层综合服务管理平台，及时反映和协调人民群众各方面各层次利益诉求。类似社区建设中的"划片而治"已经形成了"网格化管理"的基础，但目前实践中往往还存在着治理反应不及时、可用的力量手段不够集中等问题。未来的"网格化管理"一是要真正将参与社会治理的不同力量集成到同一张网格里，形成信息、资源的共享，提高协作水平和应急反应能力；二是要充分发挥基层组织覆盖面广、熟悉网格区情况的优势，通过打造基层综合服务管理平台，克服单个网格管理的缺陷，形成"网格的网格"，从而实现标本兼治的社会治理目标。

中共十八届三中全会鲜明地提出市场在资源配置中的决定性作用，而用"创新社会治理体制"来规划未来改革如何从社会体制上取得进一步突破，二者的内在是一致的：既向市场放权，也向社会放权；既解放生产力，也解放社会活力。背后的逻辑是经济发展的成果最终体现为社会的进步。

第二节　激发社会活力

贵州省黔西南州花溪乡沙坝小学地处贫困山区，交通也不方便。169名学生中有120多个因为离家太远，中午没法回家，也没有午餐可吃。2011年4月2日中午，孩子们排好队站在被改作食堂的教室门口，等待他们即将在学校吃上的第一口热饭。不一会儿，小伙伴们就三三两两围坐在一起大口大口吃起来，饭菜香味飘满了食堂。这顿热腾腾的午饭背后是满满的社会爱心。一个月前，记者邓飞在微博上呼吁为贫困地区的学生捐助免费午餐，迅速得到网友响应。随后在媒体、中国社会福利基金会等各界支持下,邓飞发起"免费午餐"计划,采取公益基金的运作方式,利用电子商务平台募集善款,并由志愿者、爱心人士、政府、媒体和公益机构等多方力量一起参与运营和监督。沙坝小学是基金资助的第一所学校。现在,在"免费午餐"的网上店铺,只要选择一款价值3元的虚拟爱心产品,点击交款、确认,一份善款便打到了"免费午餐"的官方账户上,前后用时不过3分钟。截至2013年10月,"免费午餐"总募捐额已达到6800万元,累计开餐学校350所,遍及中国21个省市自治区,受惠人数超过75000人。

21世纪以来,中国的民间社会组织发展迅猛,"免费午餐"基金只是其中的一个典型。按中国对民间社会组织的分类,在民政部门登记的社会团体、民办非企业和基金会的数量从2003年的14.2万、12.4万和954个分别增加到2012年的27.1万、22.5万和3029个。同时,民间组织的结构也发生了显著变化,基金会等资助型、支持型组织发展迅速,尤其是以企业家和富人为主体的非公募基金会几乎呈现出爆炸式增长;城市基层的社区社会组织空前活跃,社会组织网络化趋势不断加强,公益资源较多地向困难群体教育、艾滋病防治、残障服务、养老等社区服务和灾害救助等公益服务领域集中。

社会组织的快速发展离不开行政管理制度的改革。长期以来,中国对民间组织实行"双重管理"制度,社会组织要获得合法身份必须先获

得所在行业业务主管部门的审批，才能到民政部门登记管理机关申请登记。这种相对僵化的制度越来越不适应日趋活跃的民间组织开展运作的实际需要。2006年，广东省率先通过地方立法取消了行业协会的业务主管单位，为改革社会组织双重管理体制打开了突破口。2008年，深圳市开始创新社会组织登记管理体制，规定工商经济类、社会福利类、公益慈善类社会组织可直接向登记管理机关申请登记。北京市则在2009年4月1日放开成立社团的申请，社团负责人只需到北京市民政局社团办登记并递交材料，社团办随后会协调各部门审核材料，在20个工作日内给予答复。如果符合条件，就可以立即进入登记阶段，社团无需再去找主管单位挂靠。此外，北京市政府还认定了包括总工会、团委、妇联、科协、残联、侨联、文联等在内的一些"枢纽型"官方组织，准许这些组织成为社团的新"东家"。政府通过购买服务的方式为这些枢纽型官方组织注资，以便其更好地管理和服务社团。

地方政府的先行探索为在全国范围内改革双重管理制度提供了经验。2011年3月，国家在"十二五"规划纲要中明确提出"改进社会组织管理，建立健全统一登记、各司其职、协调配合、分级负责、依法监管的社会组织管理体制"。2012年，民政部启动了对跨部门、跨行业社会组织的直接登记程序，以统一直接登记、统一监管为主要特征的新体制呼之欲出。2013年3月，国务院办公厅发布《关于实施＜国务院机构改革和职能转变方案＞任务分工的通知》，明确对行业协会商会类、科技类、公益慈善类、城乡社区服务类等四类社会组织实行民政部门直接登记制度。

从地方到全国，从局部到整体，中国政府在过去五年里平稳有序地推进社会组织管理制度和方式改革，使得民间组织在社会建设中的作用越来越显著。《决定》提出，激发社会组织活力是创新社会治理体制的重要内容。政府应该正确处理与社会的关系，加快实施政社分开，推进社会组织明确权责、依法自治、发挥作用，适合由社会组织提供的公共服务和解决的事项，交由社会组织承担。学者向春玲教授认为，激发社会组织的活力就是要积极引导社会组织在社会治理中发挥协同作用，形成和政府总揽全局、把握社会建设方向的合力。

《决定》明确要支持和发展志愿服务组织，限期实现行业协会商会与行政机关真正脱钩，重点培育和优先发展行业协会商会类、科技类、公益慈善类、城乡社区服务类社会组织，成立时直接依法申请登记。事实上，行业协会商会等组织去行政化过去五年在各地已经陆续取得进展。《决定》再次强调四类社会组织可以直接申请登记，实际体现了对社会组织加强分类指导、突出发展重点的管理思路。简化登记程序、降低准入门槛为这类直接服务于经济社会的组织提供了更大的发展机会和发展空间，体现的是由严格进入向重视准入的日常管理转变，由行政控制向依法治理转变。

随着改革开放的深入和对外交往的扩大，境外社会组织在中国境内的活动日益增多，在灾难救援、环境保护等很多领域都发挥了重要作用。但除了涉外基金会，涉外社团、涉外民办非企业单位的登记管理还存在相当大的空白。例如 2009 年 12 月，云南省政府尽管颁布了管理国际NGO的系列条例，要求国际NGO必须在省级民政厅和外事部门备案，但并没有承认国际NGO的法人身份。如何妥善管理境外社会组织在华的活动，趋利避害，《决定》提出要"加强在华境外非政府组织的管理，引导它们依法开展活动"。可以预见的是，中国政府将加快制定并完善相应的政策法规，尽快把境外非政府组织纳入依法管理的轨道，引导它们以适当的方式参与到社会领域的建设中。对于危害中国国家安全和社会稳定的不法行为，政府也会制定相应法律加以防范。

第三节　正确处理矛盾

"谁影响嘉禾发展一阵子，我影响他一辈子。"

这句充满威胁意味的话写在大横幅上，成为 2004 年湖南省郴州市嘉禾县政府的拆迁标语。当时，由于要兴建一个大型商贸城，嘉禾全县动迁 7000 余人。为了加快拆迁进度，县政府下文要求机关干部、教师停职转做拆迁户亲属的思想工作，如果完不成任务将被免职或调到偏远

地区。李红梅、李小春两姐妹都在县城里当老师,她们的丈夫都是政府工作人员。因老父亲不愿意签订拆迁协议,为了不连累丈夫,姐妹俩无奈之下在同一天双双离婚。

嘉禾县政府滥用职权的做法被媒体曝光后引起了湖南省和中央政府的高度关注。时任总理温家宝在国务院常务会议上特别讨论了嘉禾拆迁事件和有关强制拆迁的问题,建设部常务副部长刘志峰在会上直截了当地说,这是一起集体滥用行政权力、违法违规、损害群众利益并造成极坏影响的事件。国务院随即派出调查组赶赴嘉禾,强力叫停侵害百姓的行为,责令县委、县政府做出深刻检讨。司法部门同时介入,原县委书记被撤职查办,接受法律制裁。在刘志峰的主持下,李红梅、李小春姐妹俩又在同一天复婚。

嘉禾事件背后围绕城市拆迁形成的政府与民众的矛盾,连同紧张的医患关系、失当的城管执法、不断拉大的贫富差距、受损的司法公信力、官员群体中出现的腐败等等,都是当前中国较为显著的社会矛盾。如何妥善处理这些矛盾,正确应对危及社会稳定的突发性事件成为从中央到地方各级政府必须面对的社会治理课题。2006年,中共十六届六中全会审议通过了《中共中央关于构建社会主义和谐社会若干重大问题的决定》,决定指出,构建社会主义和谐社会是一个不断化解社会矛盾的持续过程,执政党要深刻认识中国发展的阶段性特征,科学分析影响社会和谐的矛盾和问题及其产生的原因,更加积极主动地正视矛盾、化解矛盾,最大限度地增加和谐因素,最大限度地减少不和谐因素,不断促进社会和谐。

近年来围绕三农问题、征地拆迁、城管执法、环境保护、司法公正等出现的突发性公共事件很多都是由于民众缺乏畅通的利益诉求和话语表达渠道而引起的,在当地政府回应不及时、处理欠妥的情况下,矛盾便被进一步激化,转变为不必要的正面冲突。为了及早发现和疏导、化解矛盾,中国政府逐步改革完善行政复议制度和信访工作制度,借此为民众提供更通畅、安全、公正的表达渠道,建立起矛盾疏解和风险预警机制。

2007年，在《中华人民共和国行政复议法》的基础上，国务院制定了《行政复议法实施条例》，进一步规范行政复议制度。各地方政府根据本地实际，渐次摸索行政复议制度改革的路径。江苏省2009年对《行政复议法实施条例》中规定的对重大复杂案件可以采取听证的方式进行了进一步细化，明确了可以进行听证的案件类型和听证申请人的权利。湖北省则在同年推行行政复议首长负责制，规定各级政府及其工作部门的行政首长应该亲自听取汇报、研究案情、审查把关。2011年上海在市和区县两级政府开展行政复议委员会试点工作，成立由政府主导、社会专家学者参与的行政复议委员会。这些地方的改革探索都旨在发挥行政复议作为化解行政争议主渠道的作用，利用行政系统的监督和纠错机制听取民众的利益诉求，并保障其合法权益。

在信访制度改革上，1995年的《信访条例》是信访工作的制度基础。2008年，全国2800多名县委书记带头接访，集中化解了一批长期积累的信访问题。2009年1月，中共中央办公厅、国务院办公厅公布《关于领导干部定期接待群众来访的意见》，将领导干部信访接待实践的成功经验固定下来，上升为长效机制。2013年7月1日，国家信访局全面放开网上投诉受理的内容，网络信访逐渐成为基层民众反映诉求的首选方式，平均每个工作日受理的投诉在1200件以上。根据统计，截至2013年11月25日，国家信访局共受理网上投诉130172件，其中有具体诉求的占到93%。除却重复的和无效的投诉，约有9.5万件由国家信访局转送和交办给地方有关部门，对不予受理的投诉也及时回复告知。信访投诉人可以在网上查到办理结果。

鉴于过去已经取得的处理社会矛盾的经验，**《决定》**明确提出，创新有效预防和化解社会矛盾体制，健全重大决策社会稳定风险评估机制，建立畅通有序的诉求表达、心理干预、矛盾调处、权益保障机制，使群众问题能反映、矛盾能化解、权益有保障。社会运行中出现矛盾既不可避免，也不足为惧，正是从预防和化解矛盾中可以体现出政府治理社会的智慧。学者向春玲教授认为，创新矛盾预防和化解机制，可以整合"人民调解"、"行政调解"、"司法调解"三种资源，形成一个大调解的工作格局。

《决定》提出，改革行政复议体制，健全行政复议案件审理机制，纠正违法或不当行政行为。未来改革的突破口是强化行政复议机关的公正性和中立性，提高其在解决行政纠纷中的权威。通过收拢集中各个部门的行政复议权，成立相对独立的行政复议委员会并且实行多元化的委员会结构，按照统一受理、集中审查、分别决定的工作方式，形成政府主导、专业保障和社会参与的新机制，是一条可以探索的改革路径。

在信访工作制度改革上，《决定》要求实行网上受理信访制度，健全及时就地解决群众合理诉求机制，把涉法涉诉信访纳入法治轨道解决，建立涉法涉诉信访依法终结制度。根据国家信访局2013年11月28日召开的新闻发布会透露的信息，国家信访局将按照"畅通"、"规范"、"公开"、"有效"的原则贯彻落实《决定》精神。"畅通"就是进一步打通、拓宽信访渠道，丰富完善民生热线、视频接访、绿色邮政、信访代理等形式，在市、县两级全面实行联合接访，逐步把网上信访作为解决信访问题的主渠道。"规范"就是从程序、内容和秩序上对信访制度予以规范，提高信访工作人员依法办事的能力，进一步强化属地责任，积极引导群众以理性合法的方式逐级表达诉求。"公开"则要求大力推行"阳光信访"，增加信访工作的透明度，把受理、办理和结果等重要环节通过网络公开，正在试点的"信访事项办理群众满意度评价体系"将于2014年11月1日全面推开；对于特别复杂的信访事项的办理情况将举行听证,公开听证过程,公示听证结果。"有效"是对信访工作成效提出的要求,未来将会继续深入开展以市、县为重点的领导干部接访下访,整合资源和力量以加大解决信访突出问题的力度,开展信访事项复查复核工作,改进和完善考核方式,推动各地把工作重点放在预防和解决问题上。

第四节 保障公共安全

2013年4月当上妈妈的张芊为宝宝的哺乳问题很是发愁。在她休产假期间,母乳喂养自然不是问题。但现在婴幼儿的断奶期一般都较长,有的孩子甚至3岁多还会补充奶粉或者液体牛奶等乳制品。2008年中国多家乳企婴幼儿配方奶粉爆发"三聚氰胺"危机后,她对国产乳制品就不太放心了。身边好多当妈妈的朋友经常托人从海外代购洋奶粉,张芊原本也做好了代购的准备。不料2013年1月新西兰进口奶制品也出现了双氰胺风波,而新西兰又是很多国际大品牌奶粉的奶源地,这下张芊不知所措了……

不光是乳制品,日常生活中的很多必需品,如食用油、大米、调味料等,近年来都陆续曝出质量问题,食品加工业和餐饮业也是重灾区,常有卫生质量不过关的情况出现。关系到每个人身体健康的药品也因为生产企业的违法操作和相关监管不到位而时常出现质量问题。食品药品安全已经成为中国民众最关切的民生议题之一。

2012年4月15日,中央电视台《每周质量报告》栏目记者在浙江新昌县调查发现,当地多家药用胶囊生产企业使用来自河北等地的工业明胶作为生产原料,而原料供应厂家为了降低生产成本,则低价收购皮革厂鞣制后的皮革下脚料来生产明胶。根据《中华人民共和国药典》规定,生产药用胶囊所用的原料明胶至少应达到食用明胶标准,而行业标准则明确界定,食用明胶应当使用动物的皮骨等作为原料,严禁使用制革厂鞣制后的任何工业废料。这些用工业明胶生产出来的药用胶囊经由记者送检,查出金属铬含量超出国家标准20多倍。新昌县是中国有名

的胶囊之乡，年产胶囊一千亿粒左右，约占全国药用胶囊产量的三分之一。这些铬超标的胶囊被药品生产企业采用后，将对服药者带来巨大的健康隐患。

节目播出后的第二天，国家食品药品监督管理局发出紧急通知，要求对节目中曝光的13个药用空心胶囊产品暂停销售和使用，责成相关省市对媒体报道的药用空心胶囊铬超标情况开展监督检查和产品检验，并派出督查员赶赴现场进行监督。公安部也在4月19日召开视频会议，要求全国公安机关积极配合有关部门严密排查、严厉打击"毒胶囊"犯罪，第一时间部署涉案省市当地的公安机关介入侦查。随后，各地公安机关在侦查后立案6起，抓获犯罪嫌疑人53名，查封工业明胶和胶囊生产厂家10个，现场查扣涉案工业明胶230余吨。

对公众身体健康造成安全隐患的食品药品质量问题一再牵动社会的神经，说明相关部门的执法能力和监管力度亟待提高。与之相比，同样危及公共安全的突发性自然灾害则考验着政府的应急响应机制和协调动员能力。2013年4月20日8时02分，四川省雅安市芦山县发生7.0级地震，给当地带来巨大损失。四川省在地震发生后立即启动一级应急程序，中国地震局启动地震应急Ⅰ级响应，国家减灾委、民政部启动国家抗震救灾三级响应，公安部、国土资源部、气象局等部门也各自启动应急机制，部署救灾工作。相比五年前的汶川地震，中国政府在芦山地震中表现出更成熟的应急反应机制和更高效的灾难救援与社会动员能力。在突如其来的灾难面前，通过快速合理的部署及行动，最大程度地减小了灾难损失，保障了受灾地区的公共安全。

公共安全是社会治理的重要课题，《决定》提出健全公共安全体系，完善统一权威的食品药品安全监管机构，建立最严格的覆盖全过程的监管制度，建立食品原产地可追溯制度和质量标识制度，保障食品药品安全；深化安全生产管理体制改革，建立隐患排查治理体系和安全预防控制体系，遏制重特大安全事故；健全防灾减灾救灾体制；加强社会治安综合治理，创新立体化社会治安防控体系，依法严密防范和惩治各类违法犯罪活动。针对国际互联网给国家信息安全带来的新挑战，《决定》

提出，坚持积极利用、科学发展、依法管理、确保安全的方针，加大依法管理网络力度，加快完善互联网管理领导体制，确保国家网络和信息安全。在公共安全体系的顶层设计上，首次提出设立国家安全委员会，完善国家安全体制和国家安全战略，确保国家安全。

  对于设立"国家安全委员会"，国防大学教授公方彬认为，这是在现有体制基础上结合安全领域出现的新情况和新问题做出的制度设计。随着国内外环境的不断变化，国家安全的范围已经不局限于传统意义上的国防、军事和外交，还涉及经济、金融、能源、科技、信息、文化、社会等各个领域。借鉴他国经验设立国家安全委员会，既可以更好地维护国家安全，也是适应中国大国地位的时代举措。国家安全委员会的设置将以统筹协调和决策权威为核心定位，吸纳国防、外交、情报、财政、经贸等不同的部门职能，站在顶层设计和战略规划的高度对国家安全体制和安全战略做出整体部署，协调各个具体部门的行动，以应对国防、经济、金融、信息、生态环境、恐怖主义等多层次的安全挑战，为社会公共安全体系提供最高保障。

  公共安全是一个政府为公民提供的最基本的公共服务，也是社会保持稳定和良好运行的根本保障。一个让民众享有安全感的社会能够充分调动人的积极性，参与社会建设，献计社会治理，推动社会走上健康发展的轨道。中共十八届三中全会正是以健全公共安全体系为根本，构建安全、和谐的社会环境，通过各个方面的深入改革，指引并推动中国社会不断探索适合自身、造福人民的发展道路。

Preface

The famous British historian Arnold Joseph Toynbee once said, "For thousands of years, the Chinese have united hundreds of millions of people politically and culturally, more successfully than any other nation. Their ability in political and cultural unification has produced unparalleled success." Chinese society is formed on the basis of unification and solidarity, and often relies on top-down promotion of systematic designs unified at the political level to achieve reforms and changes. This has been proven by history, and it is an indispensable perspective for getting to know Chinese society.

Since the 3rd Plenary Session of the 11th Central Committee of the Communist Party of China in 1978, the "reform and opening-up" policy has brought dramatic changes to China's economy and society, accomplishing the development miracle that got the world's attention. But this rapid development has also brought many problems that must be addressed. In 2012, the 18th National Congress of the Communist Party of China was held and elected the new leadership of China. What is the governing idea of the new collective leadership? What is the next step of reform? People are all focused on the 3rd Plenary Session of the 18th CPC Central Committee. On November 12th, 2013, the 3rd Plenary Session passed the Decision on Major Issues Concerning Comprehensively Deepening Reforms (hereinafter referred to as the **Decision**), which is the guiding plan for China's reform and opening-up and development in the next decade. In the **Decision** it is proposed that China, at a new historical point of departure, must deepen reform in all areas and create top-level designs for accelerating development of the socialist market economy, democratic politics, advanced culture, harmonious society, and ecological civilization, thus pointing out the direction for China's future reform.

In terms of social construction, the Decision specifies that, in order to ensure that society is full of vigor, harmonious, and orderly, we must reform the income distribution system, strive for common prosperity, promote institutional innovation in social fields, carry forward equalization of basic public services, accelerate the formation of a scientific and effective social governance system, and deepen social structural reform, closely focusing on ensuring and improving the people's well-being while promoting social fairness and justice. If "harmonious and orderly" is the basic connotation of the goal of a "harmonious society" put forward in the 4th Plenary Session of the 16th CPC Central Committee, then "full of vigor" indicates that the self-regulating function of society has received unprecedented attention from the government, and society, as an organism linking politics, economy, culture, and ecological civilization, will play a greater active role in the future and will achieve harmony in its dynamic operation.

Both "full of vigor" and "harmonious and orderly" have a strong realistic pertinence. In the thirty years since the reform and opening-up, China has undergone economic and social transformation in a time of accelerating globalization. During the process of transforming from a planned economy to a market economy and from a traditional agricultural society to a modern industrial and informational society, great changes have taken place in social structure, benefit systems, social psychology, social management and so on. As society progresses, the appearance of some contradictions containing certain operating risks is inevitable. These are the consequences of social transformation, but they also constitute the starting point for the next step of social construction.

China's Social Construction will adopt a profound yet simple approach to interpret topics proposed in the **Decision** about the reform of social undertakings and innovation in the social governance system. It does not seek a large and all-encompassing perspective in narrative style; rather it sketches a direct, clear, and understandable picture of Chinese society and its future trends in light of the actual situation in the field of social construction in China. *China's Social Construction* will separate this main topic into six fields: education, employment, income, social security, healthcare, and social governance, including 21 key words. With each keyword, drawing on specific cases in Chinese social life, the process of gradual reform in social construction led by the Chinese government will be shown, and the direction of relevant supporting policies and measures will be analyzed. By proceeding from key points to the entire related area, combining narration and discussion, and emphasizing both breadth and depth, these will be easily recognized and understood by the international community.

Part 1 Education: Reform and Exploration

An old Chinese saying goes, "It takes ten years to grow a tree but a hundred years to rear a person". This means that education is a long-term process with regards to social development. China has attached great importance to education since ancient times. Since the founding of the PRC in 1949, the government has vigorously developed education and improved the illiteracy rate which once was as high as 80%. This has greatly enhanced the scientific and cultural quality of the Chinese people and provided a foundation of talent for China to compete internationally.

However, during the long-term development of the field of education, there has also been an accumulation of drawbacks. Educational resources overall are not plentiful enough. There is a lack of balance in educational resources and educational opportunities available in different places and to different groups. The "life-determining" mode of single examination is often challenged by the public, and social forces in the field of education have not been given full play.

The Chinese government has been fully aware of these drawbacks; however, the need for educational reform has also received a broad consensus in society. To teach students in accordance with their aptitude and give everyone access to education, so that everyone can have useful skills is the ideal for educational reform. In the future, China will return to person-based education and continue reform and exploration in the field.

Part 1 Education: Reform and Exploration

1. Promoting Educational Equality

"If I cannot participate in the National College Entrance Examination (NCEE) here, I will have to return to my hometown and attend school for another year." Xie Fule, who used to worry a lot about the NCEE, now is no longer bothered by this problem. When his head teacher Xu Dan told him that the next year he could take the exam in Anhui Province instead of going back to his hometown, he was relieved and felt that he could finally begin preparation for the exam without worry. Wu Yanqun, a female student from Fujian Province, had the same luck as Xie Fule: she attended school in Nanjing, and had gone back to her hometown three times to take the exam. When she learned in 2013 that she could take the exam along with other local candidates, she was finally able to relax. Xie and Wu are commonly known as "migrant students". After the reform for migrant students taking the examination in the city where they live was issued in 2013, migrant students for the first time could take the NCEE together with local candidates and pursue their "college dream".

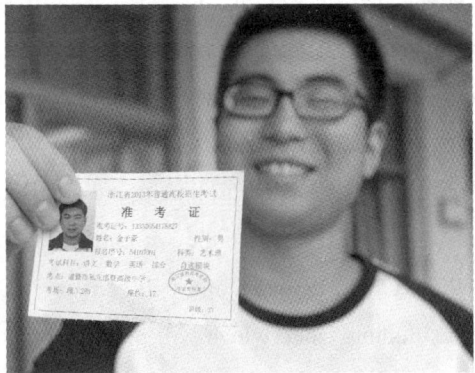

In recent years, there have been many voices calling for the reform of the National College Entrance Examination and the enabling of migrant students to take the exam where they live. During the "two sessions" (the National

People's Congress and the Chinese Political Consultative Conference) in 2012, more than 90,000 migrant parents and children jointly published an open letter. The letter points out that there currently is a floating population of 260 million, resulting in 58 million children left behind and 27 million migrant students. According to 2013 statistics, there are 13.9387 million migrant children in compulsory education. The need for reform of the NCEE to enable migrant students to take the exam in the places where they live is urgent. In March 2012, Shandong Province broke the restriction on the family registration (hukou) system for the first time to allow candidates from other places to take the National College Entrance Examination in Shandong. In September 2013, the educational department in Beijing published Measures for Children of Migrant Workers to Take the Entrance Examination for Advanced Vocational Schools in Beijing (2014). After the policy issued in 2013 allowing migrant students to take the entrance examination for secondary vocational schools in Beijing, they will have access to enrollment and admission for advanced vocational schools in 2014. The new policy of allowing children of migrant workers to take the NCEE in Guangdong will start in 2014 as well. As of November 2013, excluding Tibet, which will publish its plan by the end of the year, the other 30 provinces, autonomous regions, and municipalities that take part in the National College Entrance Examination have already released their policies regarding allowing migrant students to take the National College Entrance Examination together with local candidates. This policy is in full accordance with the goal of "vigorously promoting educational equity" as proposed in the 3rd Plenary Session of the 18th CPC Central Committee.

Regarding educational equity, the Plenary Session also noted that we must "perfect the subsidization system for students from poor families, build effective mechanisms to expand coverage of high-quality educational resources through information technology, and gradually narrow the gaps between different regions, urban and rural areas, and different schools." Guo Jie, an undergraduate student from the School of Energy and Power Engineering at Beihang University, is one who benefited from the improvement of the subsidization policy system for the students from poor families. Guo Jie, from Tibet, has nine family members but only three who work, and their annual income is about 3,000 *yuan*. He came to Beijing by way of a 45 hour train ride with less than 300 *yuan* with him. His instructor helped him finish the registration procedure and enrollment for the college through the "green channel". The college also provided him with free bedding, washbasin, thermos, and other daily necessities, which brought him much warmth. In recent years, local colleges and universities have done a lot for students from poor families, who are now enjoying their lives on campus under the increasingly sophisticated national subsidization system. Peking University's "Yanyuan Grants" will send funds in advance to the bank cards of freshmen each year, which helps with their traveling and living expenses. Renmin University of China has established a green channel for students from poor families including rapid enrollment procedure, free meal cards, free bicycles and bedding, on-site insurance for freshmen, on-site application for merit-based student loan reductions, etc. In Xi'an Jiaotong University, about 70 percent of students can receive different kinds of scholarships and grants with a total value exceeding 51 million *yuan*. The college also gives out about 3 million *yuan* in temporary difficulties grants to students from poor families each year.

In the future, improving the subsidization system for students from poor families will be the key direction for continuing educational reform in China. Zhang Li, Director of the Education Development Research Center of the Ministry of Education explains that, "For the next step of educational reform, we should effectively combine the construction of national social credit systems and individual income information systems in order to expand funding sources for students from poor families in universities and vocational colleges and allow every child to realize his value." Zhang Li also points out that with the information process speeding up, coverage of education information networks in all types of urban and rural schools and institutions must be improved; there must be constant innovation in large-scale online learning methods, and an educational information system must be created to adapt to the goals of modernization in Chinese education.

In topics related to educational equality, "the fervor for choosing only top schools" is a long-standing problem in the field of basic education, and due to a variety of objective and subjective reasons, the effectiveness of the reform has never been significant. 325,000 *yuan* is not a small amount of money to most people, but in East Jingshan Street, it can only buy one square meter of housing in the school area. The price is high because children who live here can attend Beijing No. 2 Experimental Primary School, which is said to be the best primary school in Beijing. Parents make every effort to get their children into an elite school. To this end, they make children take part in a variety of school-choosing exams.

In fact, choosing a school is choosing teachers. Teachers are key to the balanced development of compulsory education. The phenomenon of high-quality teachers flocking to high-quality schools has always existed. Also, due to the uneven distribution of educational resources, selective schools and selective classes are common in many places. The **Decision** proposes to "comprehensively arrange and strive for a balanced distribution of compulsory educational resources in urban and rural areas, and to carry out standardization of public schools and implement exchange and rotation of principals and teachers". This proposal can be viewed as a practical way to deal with the problem of choosing schools. In fact, the central government and local governments have been committed to narrowing the gap between compulsory education teachers in urban and rural areas. As early as 1999, the Decision of the CPC Central Committee and the State Council about Further Educational Reform and Well-rounded Development of Quality Education implemented relevant regulations to promote mobility between teachers in rural and urban schools, so as to improve the educational level of compulsory schooling. The Outline for the National Education Plan for 2010 and Advice of the State Council on Strengthening the Ranks of Teachers in 2012 further specified the rules and regulations for the flow of teachers. As of the end of August 2013, 22 provinces, autonomous regions, and municipalities have already issued relevant policies on teacher mobility, and have promoted the exchange of principals and teachers among schools through supporting education, pairing-assistance, rotating teaching, and other measures. For example, Beijing has shared the resource of high-quality teachers through forms of teacher workshops, mentor groups, teacher lectures, cross-school teaching, apprenticeships, etc. Again, in Hunan Province, music, physical education, and art teachers at the town level and below are not registered to any school; that is, all of them are recruited by the authority at the town level,

and they teach in towns and villages through rotating teaching.

There is only one way to remove the obstacles of achieving educational equity; namely, to deepen the reform. Vice Minister of Education Liu Limin said that according to the **Decision**, the Ministry of Education will begin the policy of entering local schools without sitting for an entrance examination, as well as a pilot policy of a district system and enrollment systems so that students complete their compulsory education at one school, and a policy of no key schools and key classes in compulsory education. The Ministry of Education has formulated Opinions on the Implementation of Entering Junior Middle Schools Locally without Entrance Examinations. For the nineteen major cities where the problem of choosing schools is prominent, the Ministry of Education will adhere to the working principle of one plan for each city, focusing on popular schools, key links, and major time periods to improve relevant policies and resolve the problem of choosing schools. Only when a new and more rational benefit system is created will the old system be really removed. When the blueprint for education reform is completed, the craze for choosing good schools will gradually become a thing of the past.

2. Reforming the Enrollment System

"The main reason for me to go to Hong Kong is not the scholarship, but the hope of learning more about Hong Kong and trying a different educational system. Universities in Hong Kong are more open and provide more freedom with more advanced and international facilities." This is how Liang Qian, who was the top scorer in humanities of the college entrance exam in Beijing but chose to study at the University of Hong Kong, describes her ideal college. The admission results of undergraduate students at the University of Hong Kong show that it received a total of 12,513 candidates from mainland China in the 2013-2014 school year. Among the 303 candidates admitted,

16 of the top scorers in the National College Entrance Exam in provinces or cities are included. The Hong Kong Polytechnic University also attracted nearly 4,000 candidates from the mainland in the same year. Universities in Hong Kong in recent years have continued to attract high-quality students from the mainland, and many of the candidates even gave up the chance to go to Tsinghua University, Peking University and other top universities back home. Students' zeal for Hong Kong's universities has made many people reflect on mainland China's current enrollment system.

Of course, reform of the enrollment system cannot be accomplished in one day. The education sector in recent years has been exploring new enrollment systems and modes, among which the autonomous enrollment policy of higher education is typical. It is also called the "university autonomous enrollment reform pilot", and was officially launched in 2003. According to Guiding Opinions on the Further Deepening of the Pilot Reform of Autonomous Enrollment Policy of Higher Education published by the Ministry of Education in 2012, autonomous enrollment mainly targets outstanding students with academic expertise and potential for innovation. It primarily uses interviews to examine students' qualities and abilities, with a written exam generally limited to two subjects. Colleges and universities are also probing into the reform of autonomous enrollment. In retrospect, the most obvious change of the autonomous enrollment reforms in 2013 is the relative weakening of "overall quality" and emphasis on "subject characteristics". For students, the written part of the test has been reduced and the proportion of interviews has increased. Some experts pointed out that this move of the Ministry of Education is due to two considerations: first, the public opinion that autonomous enrollment has become the "small National College Entrance Exam" and has increased and elevated the burden of students; and second, that universities and colleges must further clarify their selection criteria with a clear purpose and target and narrow the examination

scale, so as to improve the efficiency of talent selection.

In November 2013, Tsinghua University announced its plan to take the lead in specially implementing the autonomous enrollment policy and Peking University finished its assessment and approval of recommendations by high school principals, and the autonomous enrollment policy of higher education has gradually begun in 2014. Although as in previous years, autonomous enrollment alliances such as the "Beiyue" (consisting of Peking University and 12 other major colleges and universities), "Huayue" (Tsinghua University and 6 other major colleges and universities) and "Zhuoyue" (Beijing Institute of Technology and 8 other major colleges and universities), have not announced specific measures for 2014, more and more colleges and universities have begun to adopt science camps, autumn camps, experience camps, and other forms of testing students in addition to the written test and interview formerly used in the activities. Those who qualify will then be admitted through autonomous enrollment or will be given privileges in autonomous enrollment. These are all attempts to select students by diversified means. Chen Shuo, one candidate from Shandong, participated in the "2013 National Excellent Students 'Mathematics for the Century' Science Camp" held by Peking University and he was worried about his final test. "The test on writing ancient idioms is too hard. Many questions are beyond my knowledge. They are too weird!" He mentioned that in the comprehensive written part, there is a testing item which requires students to deduce the fifth picture on the basis of four already given. It is quite similar to the Administrative Aptitude Test for civil servants. Yu Han, admissions director of Tsinghua University, says that discipline-oriented selection of students and designing elements for assessment are the future of autonomous enrollment.

Why do colleges and universities make such great efforts in the reform of autonomous enrollment? This is because the National College Entrance Examination is significant for Chinese people. Over the years, the entrance examination for secondary school and the National College Entrance Examination are basically associated with the growth and fate of each child in China, and they are so-called "once-in-a-lifetime" examinations. Any change in these two exams will strike a sensitive nerve in the general public and will become the focus of their attention. On October 21st, 2013, the Beijing Educational Examination Authority published its reform plan for the senior high school entrance examination and the National College Entrance Examination. Highlights of the plan include reduction of the proportion of the total score made up by the subject of English and increase of the proportion of Chinese, and focus will be shifted from "key" high schools to ordinary schools. The new plan for the National College Entrance Examination to be implemented in 2016 will make adjustments to the contents, structure of papers, and subject scores. The total score for both arts and science students then will still be 750 points, but scores for the subject of Chinese will increase from 150 points to 180 points, scores for math will remain at 150 points, and scores for English will be cut from 150 points to 100 points, indicating a significant increase in Chinese and reduction in English. Meanwhile, the National College Entrance Examination will adapt to the needs of society: it will be held twice each year, and students will be allowed to participate more than once, with students' best scores being counted, and the scores will be valid for three years. Also, in 2010, the Ministry of Education and other four ministries issued Notices on Regulating Extra Point Items and Further Enhancing Management of the National College Entrance Examination to standardize the bonus score policy for the exam and other related issues. Beginning in 2014, only participants in International Olympiads qualify for recommendations; first, second and third prize winners of national Olympiads are no longer qualified, and the first prize winners of the provincial Olympiads are no longer qualified for recommendations or extra points.

In addition to the above-mentioned reforms of examinations and enrollment, the **Decision** has clarified its thoughts and increased requirements on the examination and enrollment system. Explaining the contents of the examination and enrollment system, Minister of Education Yuan Guiren says the reform of the examination and enrollment system is the key area and key link in comprehensive reform of the educational field, and a slight move in this area may affect the situation as a whole. Explorations in separation of admissions and examinations, multiple examination choices for students, the autonomous enrollment policy, organization and implementation of professional institutions, macro-management by government, and operating under social supervision are all directions for reform. So on one hand, in terms of the examination and enrollment system, we should probe into the reduction of subjects, discontinuing segregation of art and science students, and student-friendly multiple exams yearly for foreign languages in national unified examinations, and focus in particular on beginning credit transfers between ordinary colleges, vocational colleges and adult colleges in order to broaden channels for lifelong learning. On the other hand, besides the reform of the examination and enrollment system, we should promote academic proficiency tests and assessment of the overall quality in middle and high schools to build a multi-enrollment mechanism in terms of comprehensive assessment based on the National College Entrance Examination and academic proficiency tests. Liu Limin, Vice Minister of Education, revealed that in the framework of the overall plan, the Ministry of Education will publish advisories on the implementation of reforms for the junior high school entrance examination, school proficiency test, senior high school entrance examination, and the National College Entrance Examination in succession. For example, the academic school proficiency test will primarily examine the completion of high school studies, presenting test scores by "qualified" and graded levels, getting rid of the hundred-mark system so as to avoid excessive attention on scores. Students will also be able to choose to take the test in gradable subjects according to their interests, aspirations and strengths. Each subject will be tested immediately after it is finished to avoid combining three years of school into one examination.

The top-level design and supporting policies expressed in the **Decision** are probably the most systematic and comprehensive yet in educational reform. Their purpose is effectively to change the status quo of forcing all students through the one-lane road of exam-oriented education, and to promote solving the problems caused by the once-in-a-lifetime mode of examination from the ground up. Its eventual goal is to provide diverse learning options and growing patterns for millions of students, promote scientific selection of talent, maintain social equality, highlighting the concepts of "education without discrimination" and "teaching in accordance with aptitude", and finally to build a bridge for the development of talented Chinese.

3. Encouraging Private Education

"Carmela is different from other little chicks. She always wants to go to the beach, always tries to take care of the poor little black cat, always wants to…" "Little Mouse is different from other mice. He always wants

to give the elephant a vest to wear, he always wants to learn how to pick apples like the giraffes, and he always wants to…" The classroom is filled not with the sounds of a teacher lecturing or of pens scratching on paper, but of the students reading these wonderful stories and talking about their understanding. Here, reading is the core of teaching. During primary and secondary schooling, every child will read thousands of picture books and more than two hundred works of literature, and they will also act in dozens of children dramas, write poetry, do painting, listen to music, and feel a sense of self-worth. This is a "New Education Experimental Primary School", which has become a model of private education.

Another model of private education is the New Oriental Education & Technology Group. It has set up 57 schools, more than 700 learning centers, 7 industrial organizations, and 32 bookstores in 50 cities across the country. It publishes more than 12 million books each year, and has taught more than 16 million students face to face. It has changed the fate of its students. In September 2013, Michael Yu, founder of the New Oriental Group, became president of Gengdan Institute of Beijing University of Technology. New Oriental has indirectly entered the field of private university education.

Part 1　Education: Reform and Exploration

New Education and New Oriental represent the epitome of China's private education, and the development of such education is a microcosm of China's reform and opening-up process. The expansion of private education has a positive interaction with the growth of the country, and interpreting their relationship properly is also key for understanding China. In 1987, the Ministry of Education issued Certain Interim Provisions on Schools Run by Society and private education in China gained a legal basis. In 1997 the State Council promulgated the Regulations on Running Educational Institutions by Society to encourage social forces to run compulsory education institutions as a supplement to national compulsory education. But at that time social forces were still strictly controlled in running higher educational institutions. In December 2002, the National People's Congress passed the Promotion of Private Education Act, thus incorporating private education into the national plan for economic and social development, and guaranteeing autonomy in running private schools. At this time, private and public schools finally had equal legal status. The National Medium and Long-term Educational Reform and Development Project Summary released in 2010 points out the need to actively explore classifying management of for-profit and non-profit private schools, and proposes to "support private schools in innovating institutional systems and mechanisms as well as educational methods so as to improve their quality and special characteristics, and finally to develop a number of private schools of quality". The Implementation Guidelines for Encouraging and Guiding Private Capital's Entry into the Education Sector and Promoting the Sound Development of Private Education issued in 2012 is committed to equal treatment of private and public schools within the education system. In September 2013, the Legislative Affairs Office of the State Council elicited public comments on Package Revision Draft of Education Laws (Draft for Comments). Based on the Draft, it was added in the fifth article of the Promotion of Private Education Act that private schools will enjoy equal legal

status to public schools, and will enjoy corresponding preferential policies in accordance with their corporate status.

In order to more effectively promote the practice of civilian-run education reform, the Ministry of Education has carried out 12 pilot reforms throughout the country since 2011. The city of Wenzhou in Zhejiang Province conducted a pilot reform of classifying management of non-profit and for-profit private schools, and introduced a variety of corresponding policies attracting a total of 4.5 billion *yuan* of social funds in three years. According to incomplete statistics, during these three years 23 provinces have introduced policies and measures to promote the development of private education and attracted more than 50 billion *yuan* of social funds to enter the field of education. Education managed by society is gradually growing and becoming an important part in the Chinese educational field. Vice Minister of Education Lu Xin published an article under his own name on December 3rd, 2013, entitled "To Promote Sound Development of Private Education", which points out that there are 140,000 civilian-run schools of all kinds in China accommodating 39.11 million students. The proportions of students in private schools are: 50% of preschool students, 6% of elementary school students, 10% of junior high school students, 11% of secondary vocational school students, 10% of high school students, and 22% of students in higher education. Education managed by society has played an important role in enriching the supply of educational resources, providing more options, easing financial pressure, stimulating and revitalizing education, and so on.

The **Decision** explicitly requires "deepening comprehensive reform in the field of education", and specially proposes to "improve government subsidies, government procurement services, student loans, award incentives, donor incentives, and so on, to encourage social forces in running education". It can be said that private education is an important part of the field of education and has ushered in better development opportunities. Lu Xin, Vice Minister of

Education, believes that to promote education by social forces, full play must be given to the allocation role of the market for private education resources. On one hand, the government should create favorable conditions for private funds to engage in education so as to invoke the enthusiasm of social forces to run education; on the other hand, private schools should pay close attention to the needs of the market and of the masses, especially private universities and vocational schools, which need to set up and adjust teaching subjects according to regional industrial development.

Encouraging private-run education, requires collaborative promotion by government policy, institutions, society, and other areas. On the policy level, the government must actively support private education and explore ways to attract key players to private education through sole proprietorship, joint venture, cooperation, joint-stock system, etc. Meanwhile, government should timely and appropriately subsidize school construction, student training, teacher training, and loan financing for private educational institutions. On the school management system level, school administrators and core teachers must be allowed to participate in running schools using knowledge, technology, management, capital, and other means, and encourage letting the achievements of teachers and students in private education (such as patents) become sources of funding for their schools after assessment and approval. At the same time, classifying management of private schools is necessary. Classifying management is an important guarantee for the healthy development of private education, and it is a common practice around the world. The National Education Outline Plan proposed "actively exploring classifying management of for-profit and non-profit private schools", and on this basis has carried out pilot reforms of classified management. On the social level, the government should encourage industries, enterprises and other social forces to participate in the operation of public schools, and promote support and cooperation between public schools and private schools through a variety of methods such as purchase of services.

While enjoying a series of favorable policies, private schools should seek better modes of development and management, and break institutional and systematic barriers restricting the development of private education. For example, to counter drawbacks of the family-controlled, paternalistic, or experience-based management styles prominent in private education, it is necessary to strengthen the corporate management system, improve control by boards of directors or boards of supervisors, and regulate the duties and operation of these boards. Private schools should enjoy autonomy in admission, fees, curriculum, management and other aspects to safeguard their independent development in accordance with the appropriate laws and rules. Objectively speaking, acceptance of private education in Chinese society has not yet reached the expected level; thus it is imperative to accelerate the construction of a number of leading and exemplary private schools of high quality and with unique features, and to guide private schools in paying close attention to improving their standard of education so as to continuously improve schools' quality and characteristics. Lu Xin, Vice Minister of Education, also suggested that the government will speed up the process of building a coalition of non-profit private colleges, establishing a model platform for quality private universities, and organizing a number of excellent, well-managed, and well-placed private non-profit schools to give private education a good image .

The outline of private education in the **Decision** is a major step forward in Chinese educational reform and development, and it also provides good opportunities and vast space for private education. The door for policy support has been opened, and private education is in acceleration. But at the same time, the awareness of responsibility and the need for progress in private education must be strengthened in order to be on track for sound development.

Part 2 Employment: Promotion and Guarantee

Looking back on major economic crises in world history, we can always see this scene: a long queue waiting for economic relief, and the faces of the unemployed filled with sadness and anxiety. In any era, employment is crucial to people's well-being. The lack of abundant employment carries a potentially huge risk for society.

China has the world's largest population, and also the largest pressure of employment. Its rapid economic development naturally continues to provide employment opportunities, but the imbalance of supply and demand in the labor market is still very prominent. This has become the focal point for conflict currently and will continue to be so for a long period in China's future. New population entering the job market, laid-off urban workers, and surplus labor in rural areas constitute the leading players in Chinese employment. Whether they can successfully find jobs and get employed affects the stability and development of Chinese society.

The Chinese government has made great efforts continuously to broaden employment channels, increase employment opportunities, encourage individual entrepreneurship, and give support to the development of the private economy and small and medium enterprises. The introduction of various types of labor-related laws and regulations have both improved the employment rate and also constantly advanced the quality of employment.

Part 2 Employment: Promotion and Guarantee

1. Promoting Social Employment

At nine in the morning, Chen Lei arrived on time at the recruitment fair in Najie job market in Wuhan with his carefully written resume. He studies psychology at the Normal University, and despite his good grades, rich internship experience, and good communication skills, he has been repeatedly rebuffed in his quest to find a job, either getting no response after sending his resume or failing the final interview after a long process of competition. When he first began his job search, he hoped for a monthly salary of 2,000 to 3,000 *yuan* with regular working hours and vacation. But now, he would be satisfied if any company offered to hire him for a position at which he is competent. His classmates' situations are not much better; less than half of the class of 43 people has gotten offers. They, together with 6.99 million 2013 graduates nationwide, are facing the test of finding a job.

In fact, Chen Lei sees many job advertisements every day on the mobile television in the subway. Most of them are looking for security guards, cleaners, housekeepers, and other similar service workers; Chen Lei thinks he is not suitable for these jobs. But Chen Chuiwan in Shenzhen is quite satisfied with her work as a cleaner. Five years ago she was laid off from her original job, and all members of her family were suddenly in dire financial straits.

As a graduate of a vocational secondary school, and at a relatively old age, Mrs. Chen had a hard time finding a new job. The labor and social security department of Zhaoshang Sub-District Office of Shekou District in Shenzhen learned of her situation during an interview, and recommended that she go to a cleaning service company. Due to her enthusiasm in pre-job training and her excellent job performance, Mrs. Chen was sent to the cafeteria of the Sub-District Office to take charge of cooking and cleaning. Although the cleaning work is hard, Chen cherishes her hard-earned job.

Chen Lei and Chen Chuiwan are two examples of China's huge employment population. According to estimates by relevant departments, in addition to 6.99 million new college graduates, there are still 25 million more urban laborers seeking jobs in 2013. Together with surplus labor in rural areas, the population needing employment in China is equal to Canada's total population–about 34.88 million in 2012. Taking into account the slowdown of macroeconomic growth and transformation and upgrading in industry, the pressure caused by the imbalance of supply and demand in China's employment market is greater than ever before.

Under the enormous pressure caused by the employment situation, a series of policies to promote employment have been issued by the central government as well as provinces and cities. College students generally favor first-tier cities, large-scale state-owned enterprises, and jobs as civil servants; for this structural difficulty, the General Office of the State Council issued the Notice on Employment of 2013 National College Graduates which adopts the method of working along both lines: on one hand, supporting small and micro businesses through economic means such as subsidies for social security and training to attract college graduates; on the other hand, actively guiding graduate students in changing their ideas of employment and encouraging their looking for job opportunities in private enterprises, non-public economic organizations, and grass-roots public management positions in urban and rural areas. As stipulated, a small or medium enterprise can get a one-time grant of 1,000 *yuan* if it hires a new college graduate with a contract for more than one year and pays social security in accordance with the rules; small and micro businesses can get one-year subsidies for social security as well. Local governments have also extended publicity and implementation of grass-roots employment policies, including "Support and Assistance"– public support for education, agriculture, medicine, and assistance for the needy–as well as programs such as the "College Graduates as Village Officials Plan", the "College Graduates Volunteer Program in West China", etc., to encourage college students to realize their value by going to rural areas and western regions badly in need of knowledge and technology. As for graduates who have not found jobs when it comes time for them to leave college, the State Council has implemented an "employment promotion plan for unemployed graduates". They can register their name with local public employment service agencies, which provide job information, organize entrepreneurial training, provide internship opportunities, and so on, to implement one-on-one support in order to assist the graduates in finding jobs or engaging in preparation for jobs before the end of the year.

One-on-one support is the government's policy experience to help urban workers solve difficulties in re-employment. Currently, re-employment of those people is arranged by local governments according to the general local conditions. The unemployed are classified based on their situation, and the definition of people with difficulties in re-employment under various policies in various regions includes older workers, the disabled, those entitled to a minimum standard of living, the family members of revolutionary martyrs and servicemen, and single-parent families with minor children. Local public employment service agencies or sub-district offices then register the names of people meeting the criteria for management and find out their ideas for employment, desired positions, family situations, etc., and

develop personalized assistance programs using various methods including professional training, internship, and recommendation to connect them with employers. In order to ensure the effectiveness of this assistance, some local public employment service agencies or sub-district offices organize regular follow-up visits to those who have found jobs, and elicit comments from both employers and employees so they can make a more reasonable allocation of labor forces. Chen Chuiwan is one example of someone who benefited from an employment assistance policy in Shenzhen. According to the relevant data published by the municipal Human Resources and Social Security Administration, in Shenzhen 24,529 people successfully found employment with government assistance in 2012, and 24,071 formerly unemployed people found jobs in the first three quarters of 2013.

As Chinese President Xi Jinping pointed out when he visited community organizations in August 2013, the topic of employment is an eternal one, and also a challenge worldwide. China's working population increases by more than 10 million each year, and this directly affects the sustainable development and the long-term stability of the economy and society. Therefore, employment and entrepreneurship must be vigorously promoted. The **Decision** proposes that a mechanism of linking economic development and increasing employment be created, and that government accountability in promoting employment be increased. In 2013, a decline in demand for employment in all industries due to economic slowdown and an unprecedented number of college graduates led to a huge gap between supply and demand in the employment market, a situation which was also seen in 2008 during the global financial crisis. The question of how to strengthen the ability of the employment market to withstand the risks of economic downturn and build a more rational, stable and secure mechanism linking the economy and employment under the strategy of adjusting the economic structure and realizing economic transformation and advancement is the core of government accountability in promoting employment. This is because employment is not only individual market behavior; but also falls under the scope of public administration of the government. The three requirements put forward by President Xi Jinping during his visit to the community organization, namely to "concentrate on development", "effectively carry out employment and re-employment work", and that "workers must change their ideas of employment", show the relationship between the economy and employment and between government and labor on the issue of employment. The **Decision** takes development, especially economic development, as a foundation on which and key with which to solve social problems. This provides the greatest guarantee for promoting employment in society and bringing stability to the lives of the people.

With regard to employment policies, the government will conduct targeted system design according to different employment groups and different employment needs. For instance, for college graduates like Chen Lei, the two forces of the market and the government will be used–combining with advancing industry to develop more employment opportunities suitable for graduates, and also purchasing local public administration and social service positions in order to take in graduates. It can be predicted that employment support projects like the "Support and Assistance" and the "College Graduates as Village Officials Plan" will further increase in intensity and coverage, and community work will become more attractive to graduates due to increasing salary and social welfare. For example in 2013, wages for "student-official" in Beijing doubled to a level basically equal to that of civil servants, which resulted 16,000 university graduates competing for 2,400 village official position, an increase from 2.9:1 to 6.6:1. The difficulty of employment for urban workers is another focus of policy support. What laid-off individuals like Chen Chuiwan need most is the support of a public employment service system as well as unemployment insurance and labor training. China will

also improve its employment and entrepreneurship service system equally in urban and rural areas, build a lifelong vocational training system for laborers, and further give play to community employment service organizations in terms of implementation of employment promotion policies and expanding social employment. For the prevention of unemployment and promotion of employment, the government will gradually improve its monitoring and statistics system in these areas. Shanghai avoided the employment problem of 2013 partly because of its employment and unemployment warning system pioneered by the city. This system compares at least three types of data: real-time statistical data on employee recruitment and retirement in businesses, registered job seekers and the total number of positions posted by businesses, and large-scale downsizing. The government then formulates policies based on these data. For example, the "Set Sail Plan" launched in 2012 solved the employment problem for a number of long-term unemployed youth.

Employment is crucial to the people's well-being. To realize multi-level and sustainable full employment is not only an impetus for economic growth but also a fundamental way to improve people's living standards. The 3rd Plenary Session of the 18th CPC Central Committee unified development and reform in an effort to improve the welfare of the people, and in accordance will plan and implement social policies to promote employment, gather public support and consensus, bring together the market and government, and thus have the confidence to deal with every challenge brought by the employment problem.

2. Encouraging Entrepreneurship

September 24th, 2013 is an important day for Huang Yinan. That was the day she officially got her business license from the Haidian District Branch of the Beijing Administration for Industry and Commerce. Miss Huang,

Part 2 Employment: Promotion and Guarantee

beginning her third year in college, finally started her entrepreneurship after more than two months of tedious struggle. In the last two months, she visited the Human Resources and Social Security Administration twice, the Beijing Administration for Industry and Commerce seven times, the Zhongguancun Science Park Service Center once, the State Administration of Taxation once, and the Beijing Local Taxation Bureau twice, filling out no less than 50 forms, all in order to apply for the registration of her new company. It was only after she got her business license that she felt a sense of relief.

Just six months ago, those of Miss Huang's schoolmates who graduated one year before her were facing the challenge of "the hardest year for job-seeking". To solve the problem of employment for 6.99 million college graduates nationwide, a variety of polices have been issued from the central government to local governments, particularly to encourage students to be open in job-seeking and to consider starting their own businesses. But the administrative examination and approval procedures faced by Miss Huang are much too complicated, greatly increasing time and economic costs and giving a blow to the enthusiasm of entrepreneurs. The biggest headache for entrepreneurs is often the procedure for administrative examination and approval. During local surveys, Premier Li Keqiang often hears complaints from the community about the tedious procedure for administrative examination and approval, requiring dozens of official seals to be stamped for even small deals or businesses. Streamlining and decentralizing government has therefore become the key point of deepening reform of the administrative approval system to make things more convenient for entrepreneurs and provide high-quality public service.

Zhu Haitao, who runs an advertising company in Suqian, Jiangsu Province, has truly experienced the benefits of streamlined and decentralized administration. In the past year, the city of Suqian performed a thorough inspection of more than 200 administrative examination and approval

procedures and has organized more than 90 seminars of all kinds to analyze the feasibility and necessity of each one. It was found that some procedures have not been used for more than three years, there are some frequently used but lacking in effectiveness, and still others whose complicated nature hinder market development. For example, management of hydrogen balloons by the Meteorological Bureau had a direct impact on Zhu Haitao. One of the services offered by his advertising company is providing hydrogen balloons for a variety of celebrations, and information regarding the time, location, number, personnel involved, and so on had to be reported to the Meteorological Bureau for approval. For this reason Mr. Zhu had to go to the Meteorological Bureau every day. Sometimes, business was lost due to the approval procedure being too long and customers not being able to wait. After evaluation and investigation, it was realized by Suqian municipal authorities that the most important thing for these hydrogen balloons is that they be allowed to fly, and safety hazards like fire and explosion can be controlled by increasing personnel training and on-site supervision. The prior approval procedures by the Meteorological Bureau were thus suspended and now Mr. Zhu is no longer forced to go to the Meteorological Bureau every day.

After streamlining and decentralization, the number of first-level approval items in Suqian was reduced from 136 to only 57. The municipal government departments all have staff stationed in the Suqian administrative service hall to provide convenient service for citizens in a "single window" format. Entrepreneurs simply take their application materials to the service window and fill out forms one time. The relevant information is then input into a network platform for simultaneous examination and approval by different departments including industry and commerce, quality supervision, state tax, and land tax. Mrs. Zeng got all the necessary licenses to start her business in the afternoon after she had handed in the registration materials needed. Under the pre-reform approval process it would have taken one to two weeks to get all the licenses. The reform of administrative examination and approval in Suqian not only helps private entrepreneurs like Zhu Haitao in their daily business, but also saves registration time for entrepreneurs like Mrs. Zeng, thus greatly improves the efficiency of administrative services.

In addition to the reform of administrative examination and approval system, the government also has reduced operating costs through tax reduction in order to deal with the reality of entrepreneurs' insufficient capital. Due to limited funds and manpower, entrepreneurs often choose to enter the market with small and micro enterprises, on a modest scale without much investment. On July 24th, 2013, an executive meeting of the State Council regulated that, starting August 1st, small and micro enterprises with monthly sales of less than 20,000 *yuan* would temporarily be exempt from value added tax and business tax. According to this policy, such small and micro enterprises can save 600 *yuan* in taxes per month, adding up to a reduction of 7,200 *yuan* per year. The profits of small and micro enterprises are generally not high, and at a profit margin of 10% monthly profit is usually only 2,000 *yuan*. This tax reduction is thus equivalent to a gain of profit of nearly four months. To entrepreneurs preparing to enter the market, this is

a signal that more proactive policies are to come. Tax reduction means a relative increase of market efficiency, and it is beneficial for entrepreneurs in measuring risk more carefully and developing more rational and sophisticated entrepreneurship programs based on market demand and national policies to encourage entrepreneurship.

Entrepreneurship is an important means to stimulate the vitality of the market and drive employment. The **Decision** proposed improving preferential policies to support entrepreneurship, and developing a new system for government to motivate entrepreneurship, for society to support entrepreneurship, and to give laborers the courage to start businesses. The reform of the administrative examination and approval system and the effective reduction of the tax burden on small and micro enterprises are parts of this new system. The government will gradually loosen its administrative power through this and allow entrepreneurs to be able successfully to enter the market, run their businesses, and increase revenue. It can be expected that the reform of administrative examination and approval will be strengthened and its scale increased. Taking Guangdong Province as an example, in 2012 the State Council approved it to be the first to carry out pilot reforms of the administrative examination and approval system in order to accumulate experience for the promotion of the reform nationwide. A year later, in the first list of items to be reformed, 179 were cancelled, 55 were transferred to other areas, 115 were moved to lower levels, and 5 were changed to mandatory administration. In total 354 items in four categories were adjusted, accounting for more than a third of items examined before the reform. The direct beneficiaries of such sweeping reform are the private enterprises and numerous entrepreneurs in the Pearl River Delta. The experience of Guangdong will also be spread to other provinces within the next five years. It is certain that the transition of function from "management" to "service" has gained consensus from all levels of government.

Part 2 Employment: Promotion and Guarantee

Currently, the exemption of business and value added tax for small and micro enterprises has brought benefits to more than 6 million businesses around China, and the scale of this tax reduction has reached around 20 billion *yuan*. From the position of the policy, this measure will develop research into a more stable and comprehensive long-term mechanism. Many small and micro business owners say that the current threshold of tax reduction for enterprises of monthly sales of below 20,000 *yuan* is still low, and it remains difficult for small and micro enterprises of monthly sales of above 20,000 *yuan* to gain profit, but they are not included in the policy of tax reduction. How to scientifically formulate conditions for tax reduction to cover extensively the most active small and micro enterprises on the market that indeed are facing operational difficulties, while reasonably controlling the impact on revenue, is an important topic to study for the new system of encouraging entrepreneurship.

The **Decision** also particularly encourages college graduates to start their own businesses, and proposes to integrate and establish national and provincial employment and entrepreneurial funds for college graduates. College students are in a relatively special position as entrepreneurs. Having just graduated from school with limited experience, resources, and social relations, they face greater difficulties and economic risks of entrepreneurship. The integration of entrepreneurial funds directly addresses the problem of insufficient capital for college students. This policy could include financial transfers of special funds or making full use of financial leverage to let college students obtain approval or favorable interest rates on loans. In 2013, Tianjin introduced policies supporting entrepreneurship by college graduates allowing them to get small guaranteed loans up to 300,000 *yuan* with which to start their own businesses; also, new companies are exempt from administrative fees such as registration and license for the first three years. They also enjoy a certain degree of tax exemption. Huang

Yinan's funding is from a prize won at a school entrepreneurship contest, and she does not need to worry about money. But when she heard that Tianjin has such a policy, she was very envious. For more college graduates like Huang Yinan, national support of college students' entrepreneurship creates more possibilities for their life plans. This road of entrepreneurship has its bumps, but increasingly clear policy incentives and effective preferential policies are becoming boosters for each entrepreneur to realize his dreams.

3. Protecting Labor Rights

Xiaowen from Dalian is a 2012 graduate with good grades. As early as September 2011, at the beginning of the recruitment season on campus, Xiaowen agreed to be employed by Capital Aerospace Machinery Company. After the interview and physical examination, both parties signed a contract of employment intention at the end of October. In June 2012, while taking graduation pictures, Xiaowen received a call from the company telling her to go through new employee procedures and sign an official five-year contract in July, also saying they would arrange for her new job training. Everything went smoothly at first, but Xiaowen was unexpectedly dismissed after less than a month on the job. On the dismissal notice, the company politely wrote, "Because you are suffering from a depressive disorder, according to paragraph five of article two of the Reception Contract for Graduates of Higher Educational Institutions signed by yourself and the company, you do not meet the conditions for contracted employment, and the company will return your file to your university."

During the company's new employee training, Xiaowen showed some signs of depression and did not try to hide them. In June and July, she was busy with her thesis and worried about the new environment and unfamiliar workplace, so she was under a lot of stress and became a bit depressed. But she did not think it would affect her work and at least during the training period, her performance was not bad. She also actively sought psychological counseling and her symptoms gradually disappeared after the treatment. On August 6th, 2013, after unsuccessful negotiations with the company, Xiaowen took Capital Aerospace Machinery Company to court, claiming that the company had violated the equal employment rights of people with mental disorders.

In fact, Xiaowen's experience is not uncommon in the current job market. People with depression, carriers of hepatitis B, the HIV-positive, and others may not be able to pass the last barrier to employment–the health examination. It is also common for employers to set conditions for employment based on gender, family registration, college, major, and even height. Therefore, the General Office of the State Council specifically mentioned in the policy for solving the employment difficulties of 2013 college graduates that regions and relevant departments should strive to create a fair environment for employment, employers and professional intermediary institutions must not have requirements on gender, nationality, etc. for employment and job finding, and employers of college graduates are not allowed to restrict candidates by college, age, family registration, and so on. As Xiaowen said in the indictment, the law gives equal employment rights to every laborer.

As early as the People's Republic of China Labor Law implemented on January 1st, 1995, it is stipulated that laborers enjoy equal rights in employment and career choice. Article 12 further makes it clear that laborers shall not be discriminated against in employment due to their nationality, race, sex, or religious belief. Article 13 also specially stipulates that women shall enjoy equal rights as men in employment. In the Employment Promotion Law of the People's Republic of China put in effect January 1st, 2008, Article 26 is targeted at "employment discrimination", and stipulates that when an employer recruits employees, or when a job intermediary agency engages in job finding activities, it shall provide workers with equal employment opportunities and fair employment conditions and shall not have any employment discrimination. In terms of sex, family registration, and other natural attributes, or social discrimination for patients with certain diseases, the Employment Promotion Law explicitly stipulates in Article 30 that when an employer recruits employees, it shall not refuse to recruit any person under the excuse that he is a carrier of an infectious disease. The Mental Health Law of the People's Republic of China put into effect May 1st, 2013 explicitly stipulates that the legal rights and interests of people with mental disorders to education, employment, medical services, and government and non-government welfare are protected by law. Xiaowen is a typical case.

Apart from various kinds of apparent or hidden employment discrimination, the equal employment rights of laborers may also face another form of abuse. On April 24th, 2012, the Urban and Rural Citizen Insurance Administration of the Human Resources and Social Security Bureau in Lichuan, Hubei Province announced its intention to recruit two staff members from the public, and more than 20 people applied. Both staff members finally chosen were children of company employees who had direct relationships with the recruiter. This kind of "coincidence" naturally leads to questions from society. It is known colloquially as "radish recruitment"– just as the hole in which a radish grows is shaped by it, so the job openings are made especially to suit a certain candidate, and all other candidates have no chances of success. The State Council issued the Notice on Employment of 2013 National College Graduates to take on these recruitment practices, proposing to "regulate the recruitment activities of state-owned organizations, improve the recruitment system for civil servants and public institutions; look into a unified system to publish the recruitment information of state-owned organizations; strengthen the supervision of recruitment activities of state-owned enterprises; and fully implement a hierarchical and codified open recruitment system in state-owned enterprises in order to make public the information, process, and results". This regulation focusing on "openness" has attacked manipulation of job recruitment, and it endeavors to eliminate illegal activities infringing on equal employment rights through administrative and social supervision.

 The **Decision** clearly pointed out the need to regulate the employment system and to eliminate all institutional barriers and discrimination affecting equal employment, involving things such as hometown, vocation, status, gender, etc. Systems fundamentally need laws to rely on, and the Labor Law, Employment Promotion Law, Employment Contract Law, and other specialized laws in employment areas are all legal bases for standardizing the recruitment and employment system. China will further intensify legal protection and incorporate market behavior in the field of employment into the framework rule by law. It can be imagined that if there were no Mental Health Act, Xiaowen's complaint in defense of her employment rights could not have been carried out. Of course, legislation is not enough. To effectively safeguard the legitimate rights of laborers, knowledge of rights and labor law must be further increased and laborers must learn to use the law to protect themselves. In a labor market with an imbalance of supply and demand, laborers are the weaker party with respect to the employers, so it is necessary for the government to provide comprehensive legal assistance channels for disadvantaged workers. When employees like Xiaowen meet with employment discrimination and need to use legal tools to protect their individual rights, the government should provide professional and effective legal services. This is what is meant by "innovation in the mechanism for harmonizing labor relations and maintaining channels for laborers to voice their demands" mentioned in the **Decision**.

For all types of employment discrimination and non-standard recruitment practices, the government as a market regulator should take the initiative instead of being passive and make use of labor and social security departments, law associations, industry associations, the media, and other forces to explore and improve employment monitoring and supervision systems and to issue appropriate punishments for illegal activities. As some experts pointed out, cases like the above-mentioned unfair recruitment at the Human Resources and Social Security Bureau in Lichuan are mostly exposed by journalism or the media bringing it to the public's attention rather than by internal monitoring inside the administrative system, and afterwards it is rare for leaders and organizers of relevant units to be held accountable. This reveals that there are problems such as insufficient supervision and imperfect systems in the recruitment activities for civil servants and public institutions. In fact, as early as 2009, the Ministry of Human Resources and Social Security, the State Administration of Civil Service, and other departments released Measures for Handling Disciplinary and Regulatory Violations in the Recruitment Examination of Civil Servants (Trial Implementation), which set strict rules on how to deal with cheating in exams, but it does not specify the responsibility of the test organizers. This lack of accountability to some extent provides room for manipulation of recruitment results and leads to the potential for "tailor-made recruitment". This is one of the institutional barriers affecting equal employment stated in the **Decision**, and is the focus of government reform in political and social construction. The recruitment of civil servants and staff of public institutions must be done above the table. It must ensure through the establishment of an open and transparent personnel management system and effective internal and external supervision system that each candidate has equal opportunity and is able to show his talent.

In the end, labor rights protection should focus more on fairness than on efficiency, and through protection of equality an orderly and efficient talent market structure will be formed, thereby achieving a simultaneous increase of the quantity and quality of employment.

Part 3 Income: Protection and Regulation

Chinese people often paste pictures of "yearly surplus" on their doors during the New Year. These pictures show a plump, smiling baby and holding a lotus seed pod symbolizing fertility and a carp symbolizing plenty. This is an expression of the Chinese people's simple desire for a rich and abundant material life. Only when people's income has increased and they no longer have to worry about subsistence can they live decent and dignified lives.

In the past 30 years, since the reform and opening-up, China has become the world's second largest economy and broken away from poverty and backwardness. The living conditions of the Chinese people have been greatly improved and their lives are basically comfortable. On this basis, the Chinese government continues to regard increasing personal income, protecting the legitimate property of citizens, narrowing the income gap, and standardizing the pattern of income distribution as primary tasks to improve the people's livelihood. As declared by Deng Xiaoping, the chief architect of the reform and opening policy, poverty is not socialism. Achieving common prosperity is the ultimate standard to determine the success or failure of the Chinese reform and opening-up. "Ensuring that the people share in the fruits of development" is the Chinese government's solemn commitment.

Part 3 Income: Protection and Regulation

1. Standardizing the Income Distribution Pattern

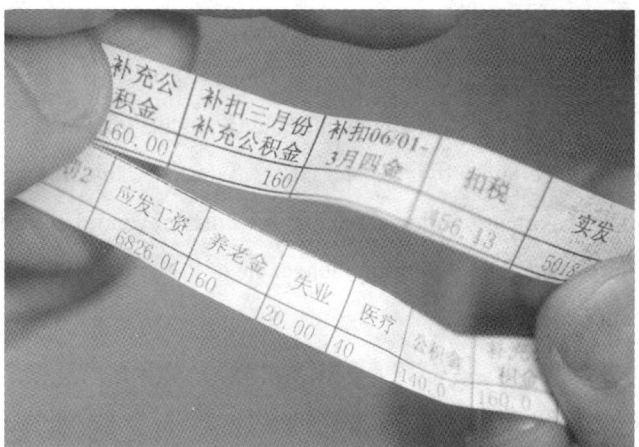

Zhang Yan is an ordinary clerk in the municipal government of Wuxi, Jiangsu Province. Beginning on April 1st, 2008, more than ten types of subsidies and allowances formerly included in her pay were reduced to just a handful: a basic salary for her position of 750 *yuan*, a work subsidy of 2,200 *yuan*, and a living subsidy of 3,100 *yuan*. Her actual income is around 4,500 *yuan* after deductions for social security, insurance, and personal income tax. That year Jiangsu Province implemented the "sunshine wage" policy to organize, consolidate, and standardize all the subsidies and allowances in the wages of civil servants and then to bring them into the open so they can be easily understood. Mrs. Zhang ended up receiving a few hundred *yuan* less than before. This action by Jiangsu Province is a response to public opinion about lack of transparency in civil servants' compensation as well as a measure to narrow the income gap among civil servants of different regions and departments.

Beijing was one of the first regions to carry out the "sunshine wage" reform. In 2004, Yang Jun, who worked at a government office in Haidian District, received his "sunshine" wages. By July of that year, there were fewer

income items on Yang Jun's wage sheet, but his total monthly salary increased by nearly 700 *yuan*. The main contents of the "sunshine wage" reform are to organize and straighten up allowances, subsidies, and bonuses, and to regulate the income of civil servants. In July 2006, China began to carry out reform of the civil service wage system around the country on the basis of experience of pilot reforms in certain provinces and cities, at the same time organizing and standardizing payment of allowances and subsidies in central authorities and municipalities. The goal is to bring the income of the country's 8 million civil servants out into the open.

In recent years, the Chinese government at the institutional level has not relaxed its reform standardizing income distribution. In February 2013, the National Development and Reform Commission, Ministry of Finance, and Ministry of Human Resources and Social Security jointly issued Opinions on Deepening Reform of the Income Distribution System, proposing that to improve income distribution, lawful income must be protected, excessively high incomes must be adjusted according to reason, side income must be effectively regulated, and illegal income must be banned. Of these, the ban on illegal income is an important part of standardizing the pattern of income distribution. The "house sister" case of 2013 falls under the ban of illegal income.

In mid-January 2013, it was posted on the Internet that Gong Ai'ai, vice president of the Shenmu County Rural Commercial Bank in Shaanxi Province owned more than 20 real estate properties in Beijing, with a total value of nearly 1 billion *yuan*. She also had a second identification card under the name of Gong Xianxia. This information soon attracted the public's attention, and Mrs. Gong was called the "house sister". Since Beijing has clear provisions restricting the purchase of real estate, the police did an in-depth investigation based on this information, and found that Mrs. Gong had actually registered four households and owned 41 housing units in Beijing with a total area of 9,666.9 square meters. On September 24th, the People's Court of Jingbian County, Shaanxi Province held a public hearing on Mrs. Gong's trial for the crimes of forging and trading official documents. Mrs. Gong had previously served as vice president of the local commercial bank, and the public have questions as to whether her enormous fortune was from legal sources and whether she had committed the crime of taking advantage of her position. Jiang Zelin, executive vice governor of Shaanxi Province, said that authorities have started investigations on the source of the so-called house sister's fortune, and the findings will be disclosed to the public truthfully.

The standardization of the pattern of income distribution requires further improving laws and regulations, speeding up system construction, and strengthening supervision and management, so as to create a system for the long term. As suggested in the **Decision**, in order to standardize the pattern of income distribution, institutional mechanisms and policy systems of income distribution regulation must be improved, an information system for personal income and property must be created, lawful income must be protected, side income must be organized and regulated, and illegal income must be banned. For example, to protect the legitimate wages of ordinary

workers, a sound corresponding security mechanism for wage payment is required. The government should put key areas and industries prone to delays in wage payment under special monitoring and improve the policy of differentiated wage deposit payment linked to the credit rating of enterprises. The administrative and judicial systems should jointly combat defaulting on paying wages, improve the processing mechanism for labor disputes, and reinforce surveillance of and compliance with labor security so as to protect the legal rights of laborers. With regard to a variety of other income sources such as subsidies, allowances and bonuses of party and government organizations, the government will further organize and standardize these and issue implementation opinions on regulating subsidies and allowances. Practical policy experience like the "sunshine wage" project, after summation and improvement, can be turned into long-term mechanisms and become standard systems for adjusting the income of civil servants in party and government organizations. Managing the income of leading cadres has also been included in the framework of standardizing the pattern of income distribution. In accordance with the Regulations Requiring Leading Cadres to Report Relevant Personal Matters, leading cadres at all levels are supervised and monitored. They must truthfully report the status of their income, housing and investments, as well as the working conditions of their spouses and children, and an investigation is done to carry out dynamic management of the reported information.

The improvement of modern payment and income monitoring systems will also be an important task for the government. The construction of a modern payment and settlement system will be accelerated by giving compensation in forms of wages, in currency, and through electronic means. The final goal of implementing a real-name policy for financial accounts, promoting spending by card, standardizing cash management, improving the invoice management and financial reimbursement systems of party and government organizations, as well as state-owned enterprises and institutions, and fully implementing a system of payment and settlement by official credit card, is to put the cash flow of individuals, corporations and public institutions under the supervision of the financial regulatory system. With the support of relevant information and network technology, the government will also integrate information resources in security, civil affairs, social security, housing, banking, tax, industry, business, and other relevant departments to establish a sound monitoring system of social credit and income information and be truly transparent and open. In this regard, the Ministry of Housing and Urban-Rural Development has been promoting the construction of a network of national housing information.

The *Analects* says that "The lord of a state or head of a family concerns himself with uneven distribution instead of scarcity." We can see that the ancient Chinese already recognized the importance of social distribution. This concept also provides the simplest political wisdom for today's social management. The goal of income distribution is to be fair, reasonable, open, and transparent. As a part of the top-level reform design by the 3rd Plenary Session of the 18th CPC Central Committee, along with other policies and various means, the Chinese government will actively and steadily solve

existing problems of income distribution, and move towards the social ideal of common prosperity.

2. Reducing the Individual Tax Burden

On September 1st, 2011, the new individual income tax law officially took effect. White-collar workers disclosed their salary sheets online one after another after getting the previous month's salary. Zhang Yu graduated from college two years ago and now is a salesman in an import and export corporation in Beijing. On his salary sheet for July, basic wages were 3,850 *yuan*, and other income was 980 *yuan* for a total of 4,830 *yuan*. After taking out insurance and housing savings fund contributions, with the personal income tax threshold at 2,000 *yuan*, he had to pay 172.23 *yuan* in taxes. On his salary sheet for September 6th, the three types of insurance (endowment, medical, and unemployment insurance) and the housing savings fund are the same for August, but as the threshold for personal income tax was raised to 3,500 *yuan*, his tax deduction is 14.17 yuan, a decrease of 158.06 *yuan*. For Mr. Zhang, who spends his entire salary each month, this amount of money is a small gain. He jokes that at least he can buy his girlfriend another dinner.

This change from 2,000 to 3,500 *yuan* is the third adjustment of the individual income tax deduction standard applicable to wages. The Individual Income Tax Law of the People's Republic of China was promulgated in 1980, and has gone through six changes, among which the threshold for individual income tax was raised from 800 *yuan* to 1,600 *yuan* in the third amendment in 2005, and in the fifth amendment in 2007 it was raised from 1,600 *yuan* to 2,000 *yuan*.

On April 20th, 2011, taking into account the increase of national income and yearly price increases, in order to reduce the burden of the low-middle income group, the State Council submitted a draft amendment of the individual income tax law to the standing committee of the National People's Congress, intending to raise the threshold for individual income tax from 2,000 to 3,000 *yuan* and reduce the corresponding tax structure from nine tax brackets to seven. After the draft was accepted on April 25th, the NPC Standing Committee solicited opinions from the public on the individual income tax law amendment. As individual income tax is related to the vital interests of every citizen, the draft greatly attracted the public's attention. The Standing Committee received over 237,000 comments in little over one month, which is the largest amount of comments on a law in recent years. The results showed that among 237,000 public comments, about 83% believed that the threshold of 3,000 *yuan* was too low. Many other comments suggested that the individual income tax should take into account differences in regional economic development and should be collected on a family basis.

On May 10th and 20th, the National People's Congress invited some experts, scholars, and representatives of the public to a discussion and listened to their views on the amendment to the individual income tax law. Representatives of the public participating in the discussion included university teachers and people in charge of financial affairs in enterprises as well as people in retail and ordinary workers from the community. Wang Yin, a worker at the Changcun Coal Mine of Lu'an Mining Industry Group in Changzhi, Shanxi Province, had done a lot of preparation before he came. He not only calculated his own income and expenditures, but also looked into the situations of his fellow workers. In addition, he checked a large number of documents on the Internet and collected the views of many people around him. He found that the current individual income tax was somewhat high for front-line workers whose monthly pay was around 3,000 to 4,500 *yuan*. He suggested a threshold of 3,000 *yuan* and effectively alleviating the tax burden on lower-middle income families by reducing tax rates; for instance, by reducing two types of rates from 5% and 10% to 2% and 5% respectively.

On the morning of June 27th, the draft was submitted to the Standing Committee for discussion again. During group discussion on that day, the Standing Committee started a heated discussion on the draft. Some members pointed out that more than 83% of the public wanted to raise the threshold, and the draft should reflect that. On June 28th and 29th, the NPC Legal Committee held meetings twice to study the deliberations from the Standing Committee members one by one, and decided that the amendment to the individual tax law is necessary. They also thought that the tax burden on the lower-middle income population could further be reduced and the function of tax to adjust income distribution could be strengthened, and suggested raising the threshold to 3,500 *yuan*. On June 30th, the Standing Committee approved the decision on modifying the individual income tax law and raising the threshold to 3,500 *yuan*, changing the nine-bracket progressive rate system to seven-bracket, and adjusting relevant levels and tax rates.

Individual income tax not only concerns national fiscal revenue but also is closely related to the wallets of ordinary people. Reasonable levying of the individual income tax on one hand can ensure that citizens fulfill tax obligations, and on the other hand can effectively reduce the tax burden and achieve income growth. The **Decision** puts emphasis on the protection of laborers' income and proposes attempting both to synchronize the growth of labor compensation with improvement in labor productivity and to increase the proportion of labor compensation in primary distribution. It also proposes to improve adjustment and redistribution mechanisms with taxation, social security, and transfer payments as the main means, and increase the power of tax adjustment. The individual income tax on wages and salaries of the vast majority of the working class is not only an issue of the country's tax system, but also of the people's livelihood, and allowing ordinary people to get real benefits is at the core of stabilizing that livelihood. The biggest beneficiaries of the new individual income tax system in 2011 are the majority of the lower-middle income group. After the individual income tax threshold rose to 3,500 *yuan*, the burden on taxpayers was generally relieved: the percentage of the working-class applicable for individual income tax declined from 28% to about 7.7% and the total population dropped from about 84 million to about 24 million. An increase of merely 1,500 *yuan* has freed 60 million people from the individual income tax burden.

Of course, being a lever with which to adjust individual income, there is still a lot to do to improve the tax system. The **Decision** points out that an individual income tax system both comprehensive and categorized must be established, and this is the future direction for reform of the individual income tax system. The current system in China is classified individual income tax system. Personal income is classified in terms of sources and characteristics, and different tax rates and fees are charged. Besides wages and salaries, there are ten other types of income, including remuneration for personal service, income from transfer or lease of property, dividend, bonus and so on. Subject to the current tax collection environment and conditions, China's tax collection for the individual income tax is mainly in the form of indirect tax, levying from income sources and withholding and remitting tax. But with the rapid economic development in the thirty years since the reform

and opening-up, the sources of individual income have diversified; thus, the biggest difficulty lies with the collection and management of incomes outside of salary withholding and remitting, particularly the diversified earnings of the high-income population. The comprehensive and categorized individual income tax system put forward in the **Decision** will be able better to address these issues, and after the introduction of differentiated deduction of tax to support parents and children, the tax burden on the working class will be further alleviated.

In general, reducing the tax burden is conducive to achieving reform of income distribution on a larger scale and at a deeper level, protecting and encouraging labor enthusiasm of society as a whole, and then increasing economic and social development.

3. Narrowing the Income Gap

Tang Bo is an ordinary worker at a motorcycle company in Chongqing. She was quite delighted when she found an increase of more than 500 *yuan* in her pay for last month. A few months ago, the labor union collected comments from front-line workers and actively appealed to the leadership of the company to raise salaries. Miss Tang works in the workshop of a branch plant for fuel tanks, and she along with her more than 90 fellow workers get a subsidy of 200 *yuan* because the irritating gases can affect their health. As the base salary for piecework increased, her income was further raised by 300 *yuan*. Compared to before, this wage adjustment is mainly targeted at front-line and low-income employees. The final result is that salaries for executives did not rise, middle leadership rose by 3%, and front-line employees rose by 18%.

Getting a raise is a hot topic on the Internet in China. "You may run faster than Liu Xiang, but you will never keep up with the consumer price index".

This sentence reflects the thoughts of the working class. Meanwhile, news and stories depicting the comparison between children in impoverished mountainous areas who cannot afford a lunch and the extravagant consumption of a few high-income groups constantly stimulates the public's mind. The income gap between different regions, different industries, and different groups is an indisputable fact, and there is a trend of further widening. In January 2013, the National Bureau of Statistics released the Gini coefficient of Chinese residents' income from 2003 to 2012, and in 2012 it was 0.474. Although it began to fall year after year from a peak of 0.491 in 2008, in the past decade the average has been high, reaching 0.482, which is higher than the internationally recognized warning line of 0.40. Narrowing the income gap so that all citizens benefit from the reform and development and instability caused by the polarization of society is prevented has become a serious issue facing the Chinese government.

The Chinese government considers the best place to start narrowing the income gap to be "adjusting the high, filling the low, expanding the middle"; that is, adjusting and controlling the basic income of high-income groups and its range of fluctuations, gradually improving the standard and growth rate of low and middle income groups, especially the low-income groups, and increasing the proportion of middle-income groups in the total population. In February 2013, the National Development and Reform Commission, the Ministry of Finance, and the Ministry of Human Resources and Social Security jointly issued Several Opinions on Deepening Reform of Income Distribution System and proposed gradually to narrow the income gap so that the divide between urban and rural areas and among various regions and residents can be effectively alleviated, the number of poor needing support can be significantly reduced, and the middle class can continue to expand.

To expand the middle class naturally requires promoting reasonable wage growth of low-middle income groups. The Opinions urges local authorities to establish wage standards and normal wage growth mechanisms which reflect the relationship between supply and demand in the labor market and the economic efficiency of enterprises, improve the system of wage guidelines, and timely adjust the minimum wage according to economic development and price changes. Taking the wage guideline system in Shenzhen as an example, in 2012, the Human Resources Department conducted a survey consisting of more than 70,000 questionnaire forms, and decided to divide monthly wage guidance into three levels: high, at 25,830 *yuan* with a yearly increase of 1.7%; medium, at 3,087 *yuan* with a yearly increase of 3.9%; and low, at 1,600 *yuan* with a yearly increase of 12.4%. The average of the three levels is 3,892 *yuan*, with a yearly increase of 17%. We can see that the growth rate of the low and medium levels is higher; this is related to the increase in the minimum wage in recent years, but also indicates that the interests of low level and low to middle-income workers have been paid more attention to in recent years. At the national level, by September 1st, 2013, 24 provinces, autonomous regions, and municipalities had raised the minimum wage. According to the Opinions, the minimum wage for the vast majority of regions should exceed 40% of the average wage of the local urban employees by 2015.

In addition, with respect to state-owned enterprises and state-holding enterprises in high-income sectors, the Opinions requires strict implementation of regulatory policies incorporating both total wages and wage levels, gradual narrowing of the income gap between sectors, establishing a differentiated wage distribution system for top executives, setting a limit on the wages of appointed top executives and making the growth rate of their wages lower than that of employees so as gradually to narrow the internal wage distribution gap in state-owned enterprises. In 2002, when China implemented the annual salary system for top executives of state-owned enterprises, it stipulated that the annual salary of top executives could not exceed 12 times the average wage. However, due to China's economic development and increase in profits of state-owned enterprises, this figure has already been surpassed. So in 2009, the central government issued the Guiding Opinions on Salary Management for Persons in Charge of Central Enterprises and specified five basic principles for the salaries of those persons: insisting on a combination of market regulation and government regulation; adhering to a combination of short-term incentives and long-term incentives; insisting on a connection between the growth rates of executive and ordinary employee salaries; and adhering to improvement of the payment system and standardization of supplementary systems such as insurance and expense accounts. The Ministry of Finance issued the Measures for Salary Management of Persons in Charge of State-Owned Financial Enterprises and State-Owned Enterprises (Draft for Comments) in February of that year, and expressly stated that the maximum allowable annual salary before tax of leaders of state-owned financial enterprises was 2.8 million *yuan*. The effects of the pay limit can be seen from the financial reports of state-owned financial enterprises released in 2012, which showed that the average salary of presidents of four state-owned commercial banks, namely the Industrial and Commercial Bank, Agricultural Bank of China, Bank of China, and China Construction Bank, was 1.04 million, equivalent to only one fourth of that of the presidents of four joint-stock banks, namely Minsheng, Ping An, China Everbright Bank and China Merchants Bank, which was 4.68 million *yuan*.

  By increasing the wages of members of low-middle income groups and limiting the wages of top executives at state-owned enterprises, the policy of "adjusting the high, filling the low, and expanding the middle" has played a certain role in narrowing the income gap. However, the Gini coefficient of 0.474 and general feelings of the public regarding the enlarging income

gap have made the government realize that narrowing the income gap will be a long-term task. The **Decision** proposes to improve the wage standard and normal wage growth mechanism, improve the minimum wage and wage payment security system, regulate excessively high incomes, raise low incomes, expand the proportion of the middle-income population, endeavor to narrow the income gap between urban and rural areas and among regions and industries, and gradually form a middle-heavy structure of income distribution. The formulation of this structure of income distribution is in direct contrast to China's current pyramid-shaped income distribution pattern. The intention is to change from the shape of "small top, big bottom" to "small ends, big middle", and this specifies the direction of narrowing the income gap. It is worth noting that the **Decision** identifies the non-public economy as an important component of the socialist market economy, giving more support in regards to protection of property rights, fair competition, and taxation, which will help to increase the level of development of the non-public economy, especially small and medium private enterprises. At the same time, small and medium private enterprises contribute a lot in employment creation, so the policy also helps to raise the wages of a wider range of ordinary workers. The combination of further development of small and medium private enterprises and the wage guideline system will accelerate the establishment of internal wage negotiation mechanisms and promote the practical effect of wage guidelines, which were not originally mandatory. As for rural residents with generally low income, the **Decision** also proscribes giving more property rights to the farmers and exploring channels for farmers to increase property income through reform of the land transfer system, marketing operations of collective economic organizations, and the reform of homestead system, etc., in order to allow farmers to profit from land appreciation. This means that the income growth of rural residents, the majority of the population, has also been included in the overall framework of the reform and development strategy of the plenary session. The concept of "filling the low" to narrow the income gap will cover a larger group of people and there will be more supporting measures.

Work for "adjusting the high" is in progress as well. In May 2013, the survey of the income of top executives of central enterprises and state-owned enterprises led by the Ministry of Human Resources and Social Security basically came to an end, and it will provide a basis for the introduction of salary reduction measures in high-income industries and for top executives of central and state-owned enterprises so as to narrow the income gap between top executives of central enterprises and state-owned enterprises, civil servants, and ordinary employees. Since most top executives of central enterprises are also administrative officials who already have sufficient insurance in retirement and annuity, their excessively high share of the market dividend of state-owned assets is not in the interest of social equality. After the 3rd Plenary Session of the 18th CPC Central Committee, pay limits for those high-income groups will become the main theme. With respect to the income of top executives of non-state-owned financial enterprises and listed companies, the government will use the market and legal methods rather than administrative intervention and limit excessively high income by means of improving corporate governance structure and strengthening supervision of boards of directors, compensation committees, and general meetings of stockholders.

In an online survey held before the 3rd Plenary Session of the 18th CPC Central Committee that was initiated by the People's Daily Online, given ten key words relating to the people's well-being, about one third of participants chose "income gap". This shows that facing the reality of the expanding income gap and making efforts to narrow it have become major expectations of the people for the next step of reform. Narrowing the income gap is the only way to form a middle-heavy structure of income distribution, cause development results to be shared by all people, and reduce risks during a time of social transition.

Part 4 Social Security: Care and Justice

"Care for the old in their last years, employ those in their prime, educate the young, and provide for widowers, widows, orphans, the childless, the handicapped, and the ill." This is an ancient Chinese depiction of an ideal world. Today, in many parts of China, elderly retired people in urban and rural areas receive a monthly pension, employees and employers pay into social security and housing savings fund together in proportion, and widows, orphans, the disabled, the unemployed, and other disadvantaged groups enjoy relief and welfare programs such as subsistence allowances granted by the government. The modern social security system has provided the Chinese people with another vision of an ideal society.

Social security is the most basic public service provided to citizens. In China, social security is often referred to as five insurances (endowment, medical, unemployment, work-related injury and maternity insurance) along with the housing savings fund. The safety net established by mobilizing the power of the state, society, and individuals together has effectively solved people's worries. In the future, China's social security system will take into account efficiency and fairness and have complete basic coverage, combination of urban and rural programs, and a multi-level structure.

Part 4 Social Security: Care and Justice

1. Coordinating Retirement Pensions

In February 2007, the former Harbor Hospital of Guangzhou was transferred from Guangzhou Port Group to Guangzhou Medical College. During the hand-over process, it was stipulated that the organizational affiliations of hospital staff retiring before July 30th, 2005 remained with the Guangzhou Port Group and they would be treated as enterprise retirees, while the organizational affiliations of those retiring after July 30th would be transferred with the hospital to Guangzhou Medical College, and they would be treated as institutional retirees. Dr. Li was a senior doctor before retirement, and because she retired before the specified time, she was treated as an enterprise retiree and got a monthly retirement pay of 2,000 *yuan*. Even after the unified pension increase for enterprise employees in China, she could only get just over 3,000 *yuan*. But her colleagues with the same title who retired in the public institution after the transfer could receive a monthly pension of more than 5,000 *yuan*, almost twice as much. Dr. Li felt uneasy about such a big difference in pension, because they had all devoted themselves equally to the hospital for several decades.

In fact, the difference between companies and public institutions has existed for a long time. Taking the current average pension in Guangzhou as an example, the lowest position of clerk in a public institution can generally obtain a pension of more than 3,000 *yuan*; cadres at the deputy section level receive more than 4,000 *yuan*, cadres at the section level receive more than 5,000 *yuan*, and cadres at the deputy department director level receive more than 7,000 *yuan*. In other words, a civil servant who remains a clerk for his entire career can still get a retirement pension two to three times that of ordinary enterprise employees.

Adopting different pension systems based on the nature of employment is referred to as the double-track system, which was a special product of the transition from a planned economy to a market economy. It was stipulated in 1992, when China reformed the pension system, that pensions of government agencies and public institutions adopt unified financial payment, with individuals paying no or little social security, while businesses adopt a contribution scheme with payment by the business and workers according to certain standards. From when the reform came into effect in 1992 until today, there has appeared a huge difference in the two pension systems. For example, public officials do not pay social security but can receive a pension at 80% of wages or higher, while urban employees' pensions are only 45% of wages.

In recent years, the state government has gradually become aware of the weaknesses of the double-track system and is now taking measures to adjust it. Since 2005, the government has improved pensions for private-sector retirees to some extent each year. On January 9th, 2013, at the State Council executive meeting, it was decided to raise the basic pension for enterprise retirees by 10% January 1st, which was the ninth consecutive increase of private sector pensions. After this increase, the national average exceeded 1,800 *yuan*. According to the data provided by the meeting, the national average monthly pension of private-sector retirees was 1,721 *yuan* in 2012, more than double the pre-adjustment 700 *yuan* in 2005. Lv Mingchang is 69 years old, and was an employee at a travel services company in Dongying, Shandong Province who retired in 2004. His pension rose from less than 700 *yuan* when he retired to 2,528 *yuan* at the end of last year. Now he is able to take care of the daily expenses of his whole family with his own pension, and his wife's entire pension can be saved.

At the same time, the state government has also gradually promoted pension reform of the other track. In February 2008, the State Council executive meeting discussed and approved in principle the Public Institution Staff Pension System Reform Pilot Program, and determined to initiate the pension reform pilot program in Shanxi, Shanghai, Zhejiang, Guangdong Provinces and the municipality of Chongqing to proceed together with the classification reform of public institutions. The core of the program is to take the pension management of enterprise employees as reference, and implement a basic endowment insurance system combining social planning and individual accounts in public institutions with the institutions and individuals paying for endowment insurance by a certain percentage proportionally, and at the same time to establish the occupational pension system as a supplement

to the basic endowment insurance. However, the reform process is not smooth; only Guangdong has made a breakthrough, with employees in both public institutions and private enterprises paying a monthly pension, but retirement benefits are still calculated in the old way, so the effect of reform is diminished.

Targeting the double-track system in its actual operation and obstacles encountered in the pilot reform of the public institution pension system, the **Decision** proposes to establish a more equal and sustainable social security system, adhere to the basic pension system combining social planning and individual accounts, and promote pension system reform in public organizations and institutions. Hu Xiaoyi, Deputy Minister of Human Resources and Social Security, publicly stated in July 2013 that the direction for the unification of the double-track system is explicit, but instead of simply transforming the retirement system of public institutions into the pension system of enterprises, there will be moves toward a common direction for reform and ultimately the double-track system will be abolished. Officials from the Ministry of Human Resources and Social Security believe that dividing public institutions into different categories and levels and reforming only one of the subcategories in the pilot reform led to a failure of building consensus and forming a joint force. After the 3rd Plenary Session of the 18th CPC Central Committee, the government will implement the reform of the social insurance system for public organizations and institutions while advancing the classification reform of public institutions. As the current retirement system for public organizations and institutions has been in place for 60 years, a smooth transition of the old system so as to reduce social shock cannot be realized unless it is carried out step by step under perfect top-level design with supporting measures in many aspects such as institutional classification, personnel system, wage distribution, financial security, and so on, and unless the effective convergence of various social insurance systems in enterprises and in public organizations and institutions is properly handled.

In addition to inequality caused by the double-track system, there is another challenge as how to realize the national coordination of the Chinese endowment system. Due to long-standing regionalized coordination of pension programs, there are great disparities in actual pension payment rates in different regions with different levels of economic development. For example, in 2011, the actual payment rate in Guangdong Province was 5.9%, while in Gansu Province it was as high as 24.5%. Such discrepancies violate the principle of fair financing for endowment insurance under the law. Regionalized coordination has also caused a structural deficit in pensions. While pension fund surpluses in Guangdong, Zhejiang, Beijing, Shanghai and other economically-developed areas are increasing, pension funds in most other central and western provinces cannot cover expenditures with contributions and can only continue operations with the help of financial subsidies. For example, in 2011, the accumulated pension fund surplus in Guangdong was more than 360 billion *yuan*, while the gap between pension revenue and expenditures in Heilongjiang and Liaoning Provinces in the same year was 18.3 billion *yuan* and 15.6 billion *yuan* respectively. Even within Guangdong Province, as there is no unified revenue or expenditure system, surplus and deficit in pension funds coexist, and the deficits of pension fund in cities and counties in northern Guangdong have to be paid off with financial assistance.

In response to this phenomenon, the **Decision** clearly states that national coordination of the basic pension system must be achieved, the principles of actuarial science must be adhered to, and the policy for transferring and renewing social insurance must be perfected. The purpose of national coordination of the basic pension system is to cause the unification of retirement pension policies of workers in enterprises all over the country. This can radically solve the problem of pension transfers of migrant workers and

protect their rights, avoiding situations like that at the end of 2007 when more than 800,000 people in Shenzhen cancelled their policies; and also expand the scale of adjustment, gradually changing the situation of unbalanced regional pension funds. However, during the process of national coordination, there will inevitably be obstruction from regions with large pension fund surpluses which are reluctant to hand them over. According to Jin Weigang, director-general of the Research Institute for Social Security at the Ministry of Human Resources and Social Security, the key to achieving national coordination is rationally allocating funding and payment obligations to central and local authorities, making clear the powers and property rights of both parties, and jointly supporting the smooth operation of the pension system and fund.

"Let the results of development benefit all the people more equally" are words with practical meaning. Both the reform of the pension system for public organizations and institutions and the national coordination of pension funds aim at establishing a fair and sustainable social security system, providing the same reliable old-age security for elderly retirees from different regions and different occupations.

2. Coping with Difficulties in an Aging Society

Although 69-year-old Mr. Hu has been retired for several years, he still maintains his daily routine just as when he was working: arriving at 8:30 in the morning and leaving at 4:30 in the afternoon. He's not going to his workplace, but to Xinjiekou nursing home near Fuchengmen, Beijing. The bus from his home to the nursing home takes four hours round-trip, but Mr. Hu makes the trip rain or shine. Xinjiekou nursing home provides a rich cultural life for its clients, and there are volunteers who teach elderly people crafts, paper-cutting, calligraphy, and even singing, which attracted Mr. Hu here as soon as he heard about it on the radio. Mr. Hu's wife passed away suddenly, leaving his home quite empty. He did not want to give up his home, so he simply applied for a day care program. He eats a twenty-*yuan* lunch every day at the nursing home and takes a nap on the bed provided. The day care center is located underground, cool in summer and warm in winter. Groups of four can also be gathered to play mahjong. Mr. Hu is very satisfied with the day care center.

However the later years of Huang Xinyun are quite different. She retired as an associate professor in a university. Having been divorced for many years, she lives alone and seldom has visitors at home. Huang was very strong when she was young and never thought about what would happen when she got old. It was not until six years ago, when she suffered from a serious illness and was faced with surgery, hospital rooms, and leg disability all day, that she suddenly felt defeated by time. Pain and loneliness often made Mrs. Huang want her life to end as soon as possible.

The different lives of Mr. Hu and Mrs. Huang are a microcosm of China's aging society. By the end of 2012, the population aged 60 years or more in China was 193.90 million, or 14.3% of the total population with an increase of 0.59% over 2011. The statistical agency expects that by 2020, the number of people over the age of 60 will reach 243 million, and by 2025 it will exceed 300 million. Aging has become a real social problem, as well as

a test of the government's ability to provide basic retirement and nursing services. Although in the past decade China established a basic social security system covering the entire society through retirement pensions, medical insurance, a minimum standard of living, and other measures, in the face of the accelerating arrival of an aging society, there is a large gap the pension system must fill both in scope and depth so as to meet the needs of normal old-age care for society's aging population.

On September 6th, 2013, the State Council issued Several Opinions on Accelerating the Development of Geriatric Care. This points out that inadequate supply of geriatric care services and products, imperfect market development, and unbalanced development in rural and urban areas are currently the most prominent problems in geriatric care. In order to achieve a geriatric care service system by 2020 based on in-home care, backed by community support, and sustained by institutional care with complete functions, appropriate scale, and coverage both of urban and rural areas, the country needs to make efforts in six areas: planning urban geriatric care services and facilities, developing a network of home care services, strengthening the establishment of care institutions, increasing rural geriatric care, expanding the geriatric service consumer market, and actively promoting the integration of healthcare and geriatric care services.

Obviously, there is still a lot of work to do, but real pressure is growing. According to a media survey conducted among people born in the 1980s, more than half of the respondents recognize the difficulty of in-home care because they live apart from their parents, have to care for multiple aging people, and they already feel pressure from life and work. Institutional geriatric service is faced with the dilemma of resource constraints. According to statistics from the Ministry of Civil Affairs, there were 44,304 geriatric service institutions of all kinds in 2012, with 4.165 million beds, thus 21.5 beds per thousand elderly, and they took in 2.936 million aging people at the end of the year. There is a huge gap between the aging population and the available service resources and capabilities provided by geriatric service institutions. Take Beijing as an example: in 2012, a reporter found from a survey that dozens of public nursing homes are completely full and people must wait to enter them. The No. 1 Social Welfare Institute has the best conditions and the largest bed shortage: it has 1,100 beds, but there are 7,000 people waiting to enter, which means that the wait for an aging person wishing to live there is 10 years.

Thus, the mobilization of social forces to participate in the geriatric care services and vigorously develop community-based care has become an important point from which to attack the pension problem. The Twelfth Five-Year Plan for Developing the Cause of Chinese Seniors in Beijing put forward a geriatric services pattern called "9064": by 2020, 90% of seniors will be supported in the family through socialized services, 6% will be supported by the community through government procurement of services, and 4% will be in care centers. Previously, Beijing had explored ways to provide a 100 *yuan* monthly pension payment voucher for seniors above 80 years of age through government procurement to meet their basic needs in terms of daily care, housekeeping services, rehabilitation, etc. Measures taking advantage of urban and rural community welfare centers, internal facilities in certain organizations, unused rooms, and other social resources to establish senior citizen dining facilities and using existing community service centers, Xingguang community senior care centers, community homes for the disabled, vocational rehabilitation centers, and other service centers to create senior care facilities have also been gradually put into operation. In October 2013, Beijing issued the Implementation Measures for Accelerating the Construction of Senior Nursing Institutions, encouraging private investment to build non-profit and for-profit senior nursing homes with land, taxes, subsidies and other means. Municipal public institutions can also be entrusted to the private sector for operation through bidding and other methods so as to realize diversified investment and operations. Establishing a senior care facility with only ten beds, as long as other qualifications are met, is also allowed; this was formerly the focus of heated discussion.

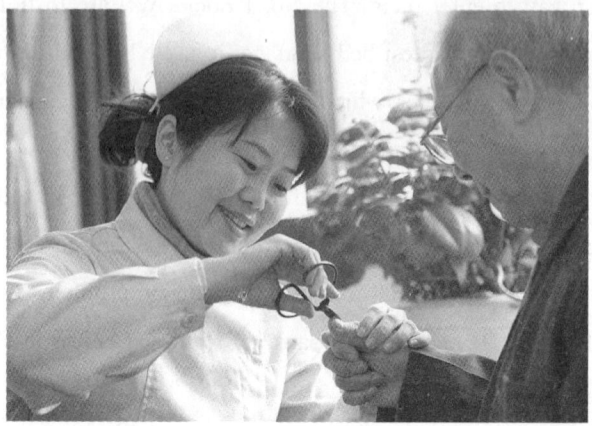

The **Decision** requires a positive response to the aging population, and accelerating the establishment of the pension system and the development of senior services industries. The basic idea of coping with the aging problem in China can be summarized as follows: the government, from the angle of public goods supply, should provide policy guidance and basic guarantees for retirement pensions and medical insurance, mobilize market and social forces to participate in the cause of senior service, and offer market products through industrialization to address the current shortage of capital, resource constraints, and underdevelopment of the senior service industry. Senior care is the duty of the government. Attracting social forces to run senior care institutions does not imply assigning the responsibility and tasks of senior care to the society. In providing basic security for senior citizens by the government, making use of social forces and attracting their participation in senior service can break the monopoly and bring in market competition, which is conducive to further improving the systematic quality.

It is foreseeable that the room shortage in senior care institutions will be difficult to change even if more capital and manpower enter the senior service industry, and it will take an even longer time to build enough senior care institutions which can coordinate senior citizens' everyday life, psychological counseling, and medical care. In this context, the integration of socialized services and in-home care has become an innovation in senior care policy, and it is not only consistent with the Chinese people's traditional mentality of home care for the elderly, but also able to meet the needs of senior citizens in a professional way. As a result, senior citizens' original social network still exists, and conflicts with children related to senior care can be greatly reduced. Trial programs in Beijing such as the pension payment voucher and senior citizen dining facilities should be encouraged. Although there have appeared many problems during the implementation of the pension payment voucher program, such as limited range of application, low degree of recognition and motivation of service providers, incapability of conversion into cash, etc., it was still a useful attempt to meet the needs of geriatric care.

With respect to emerging community senior care, many communities are short of capital, locations, and personnel. The government should conduct investigations on the status and the development of community care, and guide and help low level organizations and communities to solve problems

step by step and implement community senior services. For example, Beijing requires the construction of new residential zones to comply with certain plans and construction standards, and these must be complemented with senior care institutions which are planned, constructed and approved at the same time as the residential zone. The old town and other already existing communities without senior care institutions or whose facilities do not meet planning and construction requirements must open up senior care institutions through purchase, replacement, leasing, or other methods within the deadline.

Providing for senior citizens is a matter of survival for everyone. It is the responsibility of the government to provide a dignified, secure, and happy life for its residents when they are old. The 3rd Plenary Session of the 18th CPC Central Committee has made a positive plan for the development of the senior service industry for the purpose of coping with the wave of population aging which has already arrived and for avoiding the problem of people "getting old before getting rich".

3. Housing is Primary for Settlement

On February 6th, 2012, the traditional Chinese holiday known as the Lantern Festival took place. Zeng Tao and his wife, who had just moved into their new house before the Spring Festival, fetched his parents and their 5-year-old son so the whole family could celebrate the festival and eat dumplings. They are among the first group of residents in socialized public rental housing in Beijing. Their two-bedroom apartment of 60 square meters brought the family joy and happiness during the whole festival. Zeng Tao and his wife Song Dan had lived with his parents since they were married. After the birth of his son five years ago, the two-bedroom apartment became even more crowded. Zeng Tao was quite anxious to solve the housing problem of his five-member family. In early 2009, the total salary of Mr. and Mrs. Zeng was merely 3,000 *yuan*. Song Dan suggested applying for a two-bedroom affordable housing unit. But as there were too many families waiting for affordable housing, they did not receive any information for a long time. The couple was anxious but unable to do anything. At the end of 2011, Beijing's public rental housing began to be allocated to those who were waiting for intermediary housing. Zeng Tao and Song Dan felt that this was imperative to solving their housing problem; buying a home is a problem that could be dealt with later. So they applied for a public rental unit less than 800 meters from the subway and were able to move in to their new apartment in early 2012.

Jiang Shan from Guangxi Province is another person who was as lucky as Zeng Tao. A migrant worker in Zhengzhou, he started from the very bottom. In order to reduce the cost of living, he had to rent a small room as a place to sleep in what used to be farmland, and the environment was far from satisfactory. As the company building was clean and comfortable, he would often work until 10 at night before leaving. At that time, it was beyond his imagination that he could live in a bright and spacious home in Zhengzhou. In September 2013, he bid farewell to his humble abode and moved into public rental housing for low-income groups in Zhengzhou.

Jiang Shan's good luck should be credited to the new policy of turning

"three kinds of affordable housing into one". In March 2013, the city of Zhengzhou put forward a draft plan for turning "three kinds of affordable housing into one"; namely, to incorporate low-rent housing, affordable housing, and public rental housing into the management system of public rental housing, and emphasizing that the allocation of public rental housing should be government-led with participation from enterprises and have market rates, subsidies according to need, and separate rent and subsidies with subsidies paying first. A new managing approach of renting before owning and voluntary purchase was also explored. On July 1st, the policy of turning "three kinds of affordable housing into one" officially came into effect, and Zhengzhou became the first city to publicly announce a formal cessation of the previous affordable housing program. According to the implementation measures of the policy, after the three kinds of affordable housing were merged, the eligibility criteria do not include family registration, the maximum monthly rent is 15 *yuan* per square meter and the minimum 5 *yuan* per square meter, and tenants may enjoy preferential policy subsidies with a maximum of 70% of rent if they pay rent in accordance with the provisions. For example, for a two-bedroom house of 60 square meters, the highest possible rent is 630 *yuan* per month while the lowest is only 210 *yuan*.

Public rental housing, affordable housing, and low-rent housing are systems of providing housing launched because of the reality that after the reform of the housing system in 1998, housing prices kept rising beyond the affordability of disadvantaged families. Each of three types of housing has its own policy orientation and is targeted at different groups. Low-rent housing is guaranteed housing provided by the government to city residents with housing problems who meet the criteria for the protected minimum standard of living. It is provided by means of rent subsidies or direct allocation, and applicants generally fall under local standards for low income and average living space per person. Affordable housing is market housing in the nature of social security. It is constructed by the local government by allocating land after a national overall plan and is sold at only a small profit. The price of affordable housing is relatively modest so it is highly attractive to lower-middle income groups. But buyers also need to meet the relevant conditions and submit an application, and in many cities housing is assigned by lottery. For those families which are temporarily neither able to obtain affordable housing nor qualified for low-rent housing, the Ministry of Housing and Urban-Rural Development, together with seven other ministries including the National Development and Reform Commission, Ministry of Finance, and Ministry of Land and Resources, on June 12th, 2010 issued Guiding Opinions on Accelerating the Development of Public Rental Housing, which stipulates that local governments, as the main organizational and implementational body, should increase housing resources through new construction, renovation, acquisitions, and other means, and provide rental housing to urban lower-middle income families in need of housing, and migrant workers who are new employees or who have steady jobs and have lived in the city for a certain number of years, as well as other social groups.

Three kinds of guaranteed housing meet the housing needs of low-middle income groups. They are guided by the government, fully harness the power of the market, take into account both efficiency and fairness, and have actually solved the housing problem for a large number of urban residents in recent years. In 2013, China plans to start a new project creating 6.3 million urban affordable housing units across the country, with 4.7 million units basically completed. According to data released by the Ministry of Housing and Urban-Rural Development, by the end of November, 6.66 million units were under construction and 5.44 million units had been basically completed, exceeding the annual target task and having 1.12 trillion *yuan* in investment. To address problems of corruption and injustice during the creation of guaranteed housing, especially affordable housing, the city of Zhengzhou was

the first to take the step of turning the three kinds of affordable housing into one, by building a rent-based housing system, giving play to rent leverage, and promoting the change of concept from owning a home to having a home.

For many years, the Chinese government has made great efforts in the field of housing security. Expanding construction of guaranteed housing was mentioned in the first section of the General Office of the State Council's Opinions on Promoting the Healthy Development of the Real Estate Market published in December 2008. The **Decision** suggests improving the housing security and supply systems to meeting the country's general conditions. The major direction China's future housing supply system must take is toward providing basic guarantees by the government and meeting various needs with the market. In the construction of the housing supply system, the government needs to focus on the relationships between public services provided by the government and marketization, between the economic and social functions of housing development, between needs and possibilities, and between providing housing security and avoiding the welfare trap.

Due to the large required investments for a sound housing system and limited payment ability of public finances and land resources, the government is also considering allowing non-profit organizations to participate in the construction, operation, and management of guaranteed housing. This makes the government responsible for formulating policies and supervision, while specific projects are executed by third parties, thus not only reducing the pressure on the government to accurately grasp the scale and pace of guaranteed housing construction, but also causing construction, operation, and management to be more professional and transparent.

To attack hidden corruption and injustice in the operation of guaranteed housing programs, and especially in affordable housing, the government will establish regulatory mechanisms for accessing, using, and leaving such housing for future construction and management of affordable housing so as to conduct effective governance and to mete out punishment for illegal possession of affordable housing. In fact, Zhengzhou's policy of turning three kinds of affordable housing into one is such a measure for preventing housing security from falling into the welfare trap. Within this policy, there are no property rights associated with public rental housing, which can prevent public powers from renting in the market, and with no family registration restriction, it can be fair on a large scale. Unifying various forms of guaranteed housing into the public rental housing system can also simplify the housing system as a whole, making it easier for government regulation and public supervision and conducive to the overall design and layout of the housing supply system. The experience of Zhengzhou is very likely to spread all over the country.

Food, clothing, shelter and transportation are the basic necessities of life, and only when people have a place to live can they feel at ease. After Jiang Shan moved into his public rental apartment, he felt indeed that he was able to put down roots in the city. Therefore, a perfect housing system not only concerns personal happiness but also the stability and development of society.

4. Improving Social Security in Rural Areas

In 2009, Guo Yunhou, who lives in Haojiapo Village in Liulin County, under the city of Lvliang in Shanxi Province, received the first pension of his life. This is a big event for rural areas used to the idea that children are one's only support in old age. Mr. Guo, a lifetime farmer, never thought that he would receive money each month when he was 65 years old like urban residents. In his youth, only public officials enjoyed this treatment. With 65 *yuan* in his hand, Mr. Guo smiled contentedly. For urban residents, 65 *yuan* is hardly enough for a meal at a restaurant, but to people living in rural areas, it is enough for living expenses for a whole month. This 65 *yuan* Mr. Guo received is the new rural social pension, which includes a subsidy of 10 *yuan* paid by Liulin County and a base amount of 55 *yuan*, the minimum standard of national financial payment.

65 *yuan* not only satisfies the needs of the rural elderly in everyday life, but also enhances their well-being. Wang Ximei, from Mengpai Village, Pohu Township, Changge City of Xuchang, Henan Province, feels more dignified than before with a pension in her hand. Living in the country, she can grow grains and raise chickens spending almost nothing on eating or living; now she can buy other things with her 60 *yuan* every month and does not need to ask her children for money. When passing through small shops in the village, she can afford to buy some snacks for the children.

All these changes are derived from the pilot reform of the New Rural Social Pension System launched by the central government in 2009. Taking the pension system for workers in urban enterprises as an example, China began to explore ways to establish a pension system combining individual contributions, collective assistance, and government subsidies, so as to create a combination of social coordination and individual accounts and guarantee the basic livelihood of elderly rural residents in addition to family support, land security, social assistance and other social security policies. According to the Pilot Guidance Regarding the Development of the New Rural Social Pension System issued by the State Council, rural residents over 16 years of age (excluding students) who have not taken part in the urban pension plan can voluntarily participate in the New Rural Social Pension System. Individual contributions are divided into five grades, costing 100 *yuan*, 200 *yuan*, 300 *yuan*, 400 *yuan*, and 500 *yuan* per year. The insured can choose whatever grade is suitable to them and will gain more as they pay more. The government will pay qualified people the new rural social pension at a standard of 55 *yuan* per person per month, and local governments can also increase the basic pension standard based on actual situations. Capable village collectives should also give subsidies to the insured persons on a standard to be determined democratically by villagers at meetings organized by village committees.

The pilot program for the Opinions covers 10% of counties, cities, districts, and towns in China, and it will be gradually expanded to the whole country. It is planned to extend coverage to all qualified rural residents by 2020. Henan Province where Wang Ximei lives is a major agricultural area. By the end of September 2012, the total number of insured people there reached 46.8 million and 10.6 million people of appropriate ages received government pensions. The coverage and real security provided by the new rural social pension has radically changed the passive state of rural residents relying on the land when young and children when old, and has eliminated people's worries about their later years.

However, the greatest problem in the implementation of the New Rural

Social Pension System is the low rate of young people signing up. Scholars pointed out after research that in addition low awareness among rural residents, the major reason for this problem is that the return on the new rural social pension is not comparable to that of pension plans for enterprise workers and urban residents; the gap between it and the enterprise workers' pensions is particularly significant. Under China's current pension system, the New Rural Social Pension System is the weakest. There is also a great discrepancy in the design of pension systems for rural and urban residents. The original intention of the New Rural Social Pension System is to undo the urban-rural dual structure in the social security system, but the problem that must be solved next is how to move from full coverage to convergence with other insurances, and then to fairness in pensions.

On October 28th, 2010, the Seventeenth Meeting of the Standing Committee of the NPC discussed and approved the Social Security Law of the People's Republic of China, Article 22 of which provides that: provinces, autonomous regions, and municipalities can integrate and implement retirement pensions for urban residents and the new rural social pension based on actual conditions. The Social Security Law came into effect on July 1st, 2011. In the same year, Anhui Province announced that it would integrate the new rural social pension system with the urban residents' pension system and establish an urban and rural social pension system. One year later, Hebei Province also integrated the implementation of the two systems. After integration, the payment standard and pensions of urban and rural residents are the same, and there are ten payment grades to choose from ranging from 100 *yuan* to 1,000 *yuan* monthly.

Practices by local governments provide a realistic foundation for the integration of pensions for urban and rural residents. In January 2013, the Ministry of Human Resources and Social Security proposed to formulate and implement the convergence policy for the integration of the pension systems for urban and rural residents, and on the basis of full coverage realization of the new rural social pension and urban residents pension system 8 years ahead of schedule to promote the integration and implementation of pensions for urban and rural residents in 2013. This involves about 480 million people. The **Decision** clearly intends to integrate pension and basic medical insurance systems for urban and rural residents, and promote the coordinated development of a scheme for a minimum standard of living for rural and urban residents. The target of the **Decision** is to narrow the gap between the pension systems for urban and rural residents and intensify insurance through coordination of urban and rural development; it is also to simplify the current social security system so as to ease the integration of pensions for private-sector enterprise workers and for public organizations and institutions employees.

According to statistics from the Ministry of Human Resources and Social Security, during the first three quarters of 2013, the number of insured residents in the urban and rural social pension system had reached 490.3 million, close to one fourth of the country's total population. The pension has become the basic social security system covering the most population. To promote the implementation of the urban and rural pension system in the whole country requires not only unification throughout the country in both urban and rural areas of eligibility, payment standards, and return standards, but also allows the establishment of a multi-level and differentiated social security system based on the varying levels of regional economic development, financial revenue, construction of new villages, and personal wishes and abilities of the insured. This will expand pensions for rural residents and form pension incentives through the integration of the two systems. Only in this way can we have full and equal coverage under the urban and rural social pension system.

Part 5 Healthcare: Foundation and Security

Tremendous changes have taken place in Chinese healthcare in the 60 years since the People's Republic was founded. The average life expectancy increased from 35 in 1949 to 76 in 2011. Since the new healthcare reform in 2006, an urban and rural health insurance system has been established, which is a great achievement in the health sector. But in recent years, there exists among ordinary people a feeling that medical treatment is difficult to access and expensive. There is still a certain gap between healthcare resources as a public service and the health needs of the people, the medical insurance system needs to be enhanced in terms of scope, coordination, and security level, and there is a greater and greater call for liberalizing market access for medical and health services and the reform of the current family planning policy.

Life is the most basic human right, and the development of healthcare services and improvement of the people's health is the foundation for continuous societal progress. China's healthcare reform still needs expansion to maintain the health and safety of ordinary Chinese people.

Part 5 Healthcare: Foundation and Security

1. Establishing Nationwide Healthcare

The nationwide healthcare system first came to people's attention officially in the Opinions of the CPC Central Committee and the State Council on Deepening Reform of the Medical and Healthcare System issued in April 2009. The aim of national healthcare is to establish and improve a sound medical care system in China, so that everyone suffering from a disease will get assistance from government medical insurance. Currently, there are three kinds of basic medical insurance systems; namely, basic medical insurance for urban employees, basic medical insurance for urban residents, and the new rural cooperative medical system (NRCMS).

NRCMS benefits 900 million farmers

Tan Guangying, from Zhouping Village, Jiuwanxi Township, Zigui County, Hubei Province, who has just recovered from a serious illness, tells everyone he meets about the benefits of the NRCMS. "I did not expect that the ten or twenty *yuan* I paid earlier this year would become life-saving money for our family". The fact is that in February 2012, Tan was diagnosed with rheumatic heart disease and needed immediate surgery or there would be a risk of losing his life. After leaving the hospital upon completion of heart valve

replacement surgery, 50,000 *yuan* of the total 90,000 *yuan* medical expenses were reimbursed by cooperative medical insurance, and Tan only had to pay a little more than 40,000 *yuan*.

In October 2002, the State Council proposed in the Decision on Promoting Township Health Services gradually to establish the new rural cooperative medical system based on care for serious diseases. This system is mainly organized and guided by the government with farmers' voluntary participation. Rural Health Secretary Yang Qing said in September 2012 during an interview with www.gov.cn that by 2008, the new rural cooperative medical system gave basic coverage to rural residents; in 2012, the proportion of reimbursement within the scope of the policy for rural patients was about 75%, and the medical payment cap was not less than eight times of average farmer income, with a minimum of 60,000 *yuan*; and with the comprehensive implementation of outpatient coordination, reimbursement by medical insurance for outpatient treatment can also be applied for. Many individual farmers lack the ability to pay for treatment of serious illnesses. The National Health and Family Planning Commission and Healthcare Reform Office further extended coverage by province for 20 kinds of major diseases, including congenital heart disease for children, childhood leukemia, uremia (mid to late stage renal disease), apoplexy, and coronary heart disease. Xiao Jia, a farmer from Guanyin Village, Jinxi Town, Taihu County, Anhui Province, suffered from aplastic anemia and was hospitalized from March to September 2012. His total medical expenses were 680,300 *yuan*, of which 488,000 *yuan* was paid by NRCMS.

This new rural medical system made for China's national condition can be more directly understood from numbers. In 2003, when NRCMS was launched, only 70 million farmers participated in it, but in 2008, 91.5% of farmers nationwide joined the system, amounting to almost full coverage. According to relevant statistics, by the end of June 2013, the number of participants in the new rural cooperative medical insurance system was 802 million, with a participation rate of 99%. There is no doubt that this is the largest healthcare system in the world. NRCMS is funded jointly by individuals, collectives, and the government, and the per capita funding standard rises with the increasing Chinese national strength. In 2012, per capita funding for NRCMS reached 308.5 *yuan*, and in 2013 it will increase to 340 *yuan*, and all levels of government subsidies will rise to 280 *yuan* per capita. It is expected that by 2015, government subsidies for each person can reach 360 *yuan* per person per year. With increasing levels of funding, outpatient and inpatient reimbursement levels will rise, and farmers will enjoy more actual coverage.

Serious disease insurance prevent poverty caused by disease

Fang Wenbao, from Tianran Village, Xinzhou Town, Yingjiang District, Anqing City, Anhui Province, has suffered from diabetes for many years. He has been treated with Novolin injections, and each injection costs 55 *yuan*, but he only needs to pay 22 yuan because extended coverage for serious disease pays 60%. The 33 *yuan* reduction for each injection is not a lot, but he uses the injection through the year, and it is not a small sum when added up. Jia Lianying and her family, from Jiangning District, Nanjing, Jiangsu

Province, also benefited from the policy. She was diagnosed with lung cancer in November 2011, and the total reimbursement from extended coverage for serious disease was 221,300 *yuan* in two years. This saved her family from poverty caused by medical bills.

In 2012, the National Development and Reform Commission and five other departments issued the Guidance on the Major Illness Medical Insurance for Residents in Rural and Urban Areas, requiring the promotion of the major disease coverage pilot program. The **Decision** makes explicit the need to increase and improve medical insurance for major diseases and the relief system. The improvement of major disease insurance and the relief system is also something the public expects to be one of the focuses of healthcare reform in the future. Since 2012 when extended coverage for serious diseases and insurance for serious diseases were comprehensively launched, the actual reimbursement of hospitalization costs for major diseases has reached or surpassed 70% of the original medical bills. By October 2013, 23 provinces, autonomous regions, and municipalities had begun to implement serious disease insurance programs and 120 cities were designated to do pilot programs. In November 2013, six ministries including the Development and Reform Commission, the National Health and Family Planning Commission, and the Ministry of Finance issued guiding opinions to introduce market mechanisms to establish serious disease insurance system in order to avoid poverty caused by major illnesses for people covered under medical insurance for urban residents and the NRCMS. The intended users of serious disease insurance are people covered by medical insurance for urban residents or the NRCMS, and it is funded by those two systems without any additional burden on individuals. Since 2013, the focus of rural medical care has also begun to shift toward major diseases and the actual reimbursement for medical bills from major diseases has increased to 70%. For people qualified for poverty relief, the Ministry of Civil Affairs will give further compensation of 20% in the form of medical aid funds, so that the total reimbursement is not less than 90%.

Long-distance settlement of healthcare insurance in line with public will

Zhang Guizhi retired in Changchun, Jilin Province, and afterward settled in Haikou, Hainan Province in 1997. Because she suffers from certain illnesses, she has high monthly medical costs. She is used to sending her medical bills to her former employer for reimbursement once they total 5,000 *yuan*, and she must wait for about a month before the reimbursement arrives. In 2010, when long-distance transaction of healthcare insurance began in Hainan, she did not hesitate to apply for a long-distance medical insurance card. On March 26th, 2011, she was able to be hospitalized in a fixed hospital in Haikou using that card and without paying a deposit.

China has long managed medical insurance regionally; medical institutions in other areas were not restrained or affected by local healthcare policies of the insured person, so a patient with insurance from town A could not be reimbursed by insurance for treatment in town B. With China's economic development, population mobility between various cities is increasing, and there is more and more demand for the acceptance of insurance from other regions. In 2009, soon after the issuance of the Opinions on Deepening Reform of the Medical and Healthcare System, the country announced the Plan to Reform Important Areas in the Healthcare System (2009-2011) to accelerate the establishment of multi-region transactions for medical insurance, which is of most concern to many people. Zhang Guizhi is a beneficiary of this policy.

By August 2013, the medical insurance of 86% of the country's workers and 83% of urban residents with insurance had care coordinated at the city level, the four independently-administered municipalities, Hainan Province, and the Tibet Autonomous Region achieved provincial-level coordination, and the NRCMS is mainly based on county-level coordination. In other words, China's three basic medical insurance systems–medical insurance for urban workers, medical insurance for urban residents, and the new rural cooperative medical system–have basically achieved real-time comprehensive inter-regional settlement of compensation. Meanwhile, through the establishment of a provincial settlement platform, many provinces are also actively promoting real-time inter-region settlement within the province. Among them, 90% of the counties, cities, and districts that take part in the NRCMS as well as medical insurance for workers and urban residents in eight provinces, autonomous regions, and municipalities all implemented inter-regional real-time settlement within the province. With respect to cross-provincial settlement of medical insurance, exploration of a variety of methods is being carried out around China. For example, two regions can sign an agreement according to which the medical expenses shall be settled. This is a method adopted by Hainan, Shanghai and other provinces, and the lives of people like Zhang Guizhi have become convenient thanks to this. The NRCMS is actively building a national information platform which has connected the Beijing, Inner Mongolia, Jilin, and other nine provincial-level platforms with 29 major medical institutions, laying a foundation for inter-regional real-time settlement.

The National Health and Family Planning Commission issued in July 2013 the Plan to Deepen Reform of the Medical and Health Care for 2013, which stresses the need to vigorously promote the inter-regional settlement of medical insurance, gradually carry out provincial-level and inter-regional real-time settlement of medical insurance, and carry out pilot projects in some provinces. Of course, it is still a big challenge for cities with huge regional differences to achieve networking of medical insurance settlements. The experience of Hainan province is worth learning from.

Successful cases of free medical care

During the process of full implementation of the nationwide healthcare system, there was an exciting experiment–free medical care–in Shenmu County, located in northern Shaanxi Province. On March 1st, 2009, the county government began to implement free medical care, and 400,000 people in the county began to enjoy a 300,000 *yuan* maximum yearly reimbursement  of medical expenses. Anyone who has a family registration in Shenmu and receives medical treatment in designated medical institutions will benefit from the system. The idea for free medical care is clear: to continue reform of the healthcare system in a way with the greatest recognition and the most workable pattern and let everyone enjoy unified healthcare and equal social welfare, giving patients with serious diseases chances to get a second life. According to statistics from the Shenmu County Health Bureau, the total cost of free medical care in 2012 was 249 million *yuan*, reimbursement of medical expenses for hospitalization added up to 200 million *yuan*, and the reimbursement rate per capita within the county was up to 84.63%. Total hospitalized patients reached 46,084, with rural residents accounting for 93.39% of that. These statistics show that the trial of free medical care was successful, and ordinary people have obtained real benefits from it. Although the Shenmu model is an individual case, its bold attempt provides useful experience for the promotion and implementation of the new medical reform. The continuation of the Shenmu model is worth looking forward to.

2. Improving the Medical Service System

Mrs. Zhong, a farmer hospitalized in the hospital in Pingshang Town, Xinshao County, Hunan Province, says that after the conditions in the local clinic were improved, she stopped going to the county town and the city to see a doctor. People's traditional idea about rural health clinics is that they are obsolescent and crude. But the health center in Pingshang Village has all the clinical departments, and it is equipped with a 500 mA x-ray machine, imported color B-scan ultrasound machine, trace detection, central oxygen supply, and other high-quality equipment, eliminating the outdated impression people had about rural community medical clinics.

The medical and health service system is huge. By the end of July 2013, the number of healthcare institutions nationwide reached 961,000, including 24,000 hospitals, 922,000 primary care institutions, 12,000 professional public health institutions, and 2,000 other institutions. Among primary health care institutions, there are 34,000 community health service centers or stations, 37,000 township hospitals, 656,000 village clinics, and 183,000 clinics. In this huge system, primary care institutions, the weakest link, have the greatest number. Thus improving primary care services has been the focus of healthcare reform. Since 2006, when the new medical reform was started, a lot of manpower, materials, and funds have been invested in communities, and primary care institutions have changed dramatically.

Although the achievements in primary care reform are apparent, there is still a lot to improve. For example, while equipment becomes more and more complete, most primary health care institutions still lack sufficient medical personnel. Most high-quality medical resources are concentrated in large hospitals, and primary community hospitals are short, so large hospitals are still overcrowded while community hospitals receive only a small number of patients. Therefore, the **Decision** emphasizes the need to deepen comprehensive reform of primary care institutions, and to improve networks and systems of urban and rural primary care services. It also clearly specifies the next focus of reform: "Improve the reasonable diagnosis and treatment model, and establish a contractual service relationship between community doctors and local residents. Make full use of information technology to promote the equal outward flow of high-quality medical resources. Strengthen the integration of regional public health services".

The hierarchical treatment model refers to the scientific treatment model through which rational allocation of medical resources to large hospitals and community hospitals allows minor illnesses to be treated within the community, and patients with major diseases are transferred to large hospitals for treatment, returning to community hospitals for rehabilitation. Only when community hospitals and large hospitals are assigned differentiated responsibilities can the flow of patients be reasonably guided. For example, Punan Hospital in Shanghai and its six surrounding community health centers are connected to form a "combination of convenience", and open an express lane for connecting home sickbeds to hospital rooms as a complement to community health service centers. Two-way referral and the "express lane" help to alleviate the shortage of community health service centers in terms of personnel, equipment, medical technology, etc. This is a typical practice of the hierarchical treatment model.

Having a contractual service relationship between community doctors and residents means that the two parties sign a contract for health management and healthcare services and then work together to manage the health of residents. Since 2007, family doctors have begun to appear in Beijing, Shanghai, Guangzhou, and other developed cities. In Beijing, more than 3,000 family-doctor mode service teams have been set up, and have signed contracts with 3.61 million families with a total population of 7.59 million people. The contracting rate for important groups such as people over 65 years old and patients with certain four chronic diseases has exceeded 70%.

"China will build sharable electronic medical records and a basic data repository for health records", said Wang Cai, deputy director of Statistical Information Center, National Health and Family Planning Commission. He added, "Healthcare information technology is an important support system for implementing healthcare reform, improving health care service quality and efficiency, reducing medicine costs, and promoting equal access to basic health care services." At present, Xiamen is the only Chinese city which has successfully created electronic health records for residents and established the sharing of relevant health information resources throughout the whole city. Xiamen creates health records for residents with their social security card as identification. Residents can use the social security card to make an appointment for treatment or check the results of examinations over the Internet, or with mobile phones or interactive television. All health information, illnesses to be treated, and test results from the time a participant is born are entered into the database. Various medical institutions are able to share, record, and edit electronic medical records, and the practice of one record per hospital has changed to one card for the whole city. The use of information technology in medical records not only eliminates the tedious process going in person to the hospital but also effectively reduces the difficulty of making appointments.

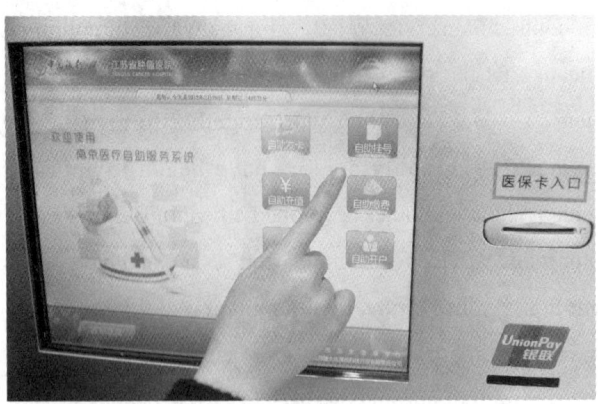

Zigui County in Hubei Province is a typical case of informationalization in rural areas. It has informationalized village health clinics in the NRCMS at 280 selected medical institutions, covering the provincial, city, county, township, and village levels, and it has also fully implemented electronic health records for local residents, digitalized medical records and prescriptions, and built a regional health information management platform covering basic medicinal management, public health services, medical services management, comprehensive health management, and the NRCMS.

The *Lancet*, a British authoritative medical journal commented, "The objective and overall strategy of the Chinese medical reform are worthy of emulation. China has made great achievements in providing equal, affordable basic medical services, which will not only affect the future of China but also the global medical system."

3. Encouraging Private Investment in the Medical Sector

In June 2012, after more than ten years of preparation, the construction of Peking University International Hospital in Zhongguancun Life Science Park was completed, and it will begin trial operation in 2014. Different from ordinary public hospitals, Peking University International Hospital is funded by a private enterprise and is affiliated with the Peking University Medical Group, with Founder Group and Peking University holding 70% and 30% stock rights respectively. The total investment in this long-planned large-scale non-profit medical institution is over 4.5 billion *yuan*, and it has 36 medical centers, 49 departments, and 1,800 beds, breaking the record for Asia's largest single medical building. As a pilot project for private investment in the medical sector in Beijing, Peking University International Hospital will accept medical insurance and residents can enjoy the same medical reimbursements as in public hospitals. It has an advantage over many other

private hospitals and can attract more ordinary citizens for medical treatment. In the next five years, the China Development Bank will provide 10 billion *yuan* as a cooperation fund for Peking University Medical Group for its participation in the reform of public hospitals and the development of the medical and healthcare industries.

In 2006, China's new medical reform was initiated. After three years of deliberation, the State Council promulgated the Opinions on Deepening Reform of the Medical and Healthcare System and the Implementation Plans on Deepening Reform of the Medical and Healthcare System (2009-2011), proposing "to encourage and guide social capital in the development of medical and healthcare services. The development of non-public medical institutions shall be actively promoted so as to form a medical system with diversified investors and investment means". At the end of 2010, the State Council issued again the Opinions on Further Encouraging and Guiding the Establishment of Medical Institutions with Private Capital, encouraging the private sector to run medical institutions. The Twelfth National Five-year Plan for medical reform emphasizes that by 2015, beds and services in non-public medical institutions should amount to about 20% of the total. With the promotion of the new medical reform, people's understanding of private capital in the medical sector is coming together. In 2012, the Beijing Municipal Government for the first time released encouraging policies for private investment in the medical sector. This new policy is referred to as "Beijing's 18 Measures". It shows that Beijing will allow private capital to run medical institutions of all levels, new hospitals will give priority to private capital, and the policy for government-run and private hospitals will be equal.

Practice has proven that private investment in the medical sector is conducive to increasing medical and health resources, increasing service supply, and improving the efficiency and quality of medical care services.

Another case of private investment in the medical sector–the Smile Angel Children's Hospital–can be taken as an example. On December 23rd, 2011, the Smile Angel Children's Hospital was established as a private non-profit hospital. "There is no overpowering smell of Lysol. There are over 50 multi-functional beds under the same roof. And there are four modern operating rooms with laminar air flow and more than 120 doctors and nurses." Liu Yanqun, the executive president of the Smile Angel Children's Hospital thus described it. The responsible party in Beijing Municipal Health Bureau holds that Smile Angel Children's Hospital "is a useful exploration of hospitals run with charitable donations. Meanwhile, it provides good medical and healthcare services for children in the community".

The **Decision** further elaborates on utilizing private investment in the medical sector, encouraging private investment in the medical sector and giving priority to supporting non-profit hospitals run by private investors. Private capital can be directly invested in areas which have diverse service needs but scarce resources, and participate in the restructuring and reorganization of public hospitals by various means. Doctors with a license are allowed to work in more than one hospital, and medical insurance may cover private hospitals.

Sun Zhigang, director of the Healthcare Reform Office of the State Council, interprets the direction of reform regarding encouraging private investment in the medical sector as specified in the **Decision** as having the following three aspects:

The first is to give priority to supporting non-profit hospitals run by private investors. Preferential support should be given to investment in non-profit medical institutions with private capital. In particular, social forces should be encouraged to establish charitable medical institutions, or provide charitable donations to medical assistance and medical institutions. Smile Angel Children's Hospital falls into this category.

The second is for private capital to be directly invested into areas with diverse service needs but scarce resources. Non-public medical institutions should be encouraged to develop into high-quality, large-scale medical groups, and develop new health services, such as medical rehabilitation, nursing for the elderly, health counseling, plastic and aesthetic surgery, fitness and health programs, and so on. Mary's Hospital for Women and Infants in Beijing, Beijing Songtang Hospital, and Zhongcun Retired Cadres Clinic in Nanhai District, Foshan are all good examples of private medical institutions with high credit ratings offering diverse services.

The third is to allow social forces to participate in the restructuring and reorganization of public hospitals by various means. On the premises of ensuring no loss of state assets, private capital should be supported in participating in the restructuring and reorganization of public hospitals, including state-owned enterprises, through cooperation, merger, and acquisition in order to increase the vitality of public hospitals. The participation of private capital in the public hospital system has enriched and diversified public hospital reform, and to some extent also contributes to the promotion of such reform. The public hospital is the main part of China's medical service system, playing a pivotal role in guaranteeing basic care and as such is one of the public's focuses in the new health care reform. With the deepening of public hospital reform, the difficulties faced by the reform are increasing. But the participation of social forces and private capital can give full play to the roles of market players and social organizations, allowing them to participate in management of public health care in forms of trusteeship and stock ownership, etc., and to form the health service mechanism involving multiple parties, thereby increasing the vitality of public hospitals and accelerating the reform process. For example, in 2011, Beijing Jingmei Group General Hospital was entrusted by the Mentougou District Government in Beijing to Phoenix United Hospital for trusteeship, and the annual income of Beijing Jingmei Group General Hospital in that year rose by 20%.

The **Decision** allows licensed doctors to work in more than one hospital, and it also highlights encouraging private investment in the medical sector. In 2012, the Qingdao Municipal Health Bureau issued the Qingdao Physician Multi-Site Work Pilot Program, and defined multi-site working as such: physicians who have a license in clinical, oral, or traditional Chinese medicine can work in two to three different medical institutions if they obtain the approval of the original medical institution of registration and then register with the relevant healthcare administrative departments. Allowing licensed doctors to work in more than one hospital can contribute to the outward flow of high-quality medical resources. Doctors in large hospitals can move to lower-level medical institutions to meet the multiple needs of patients and to facilitate patients' access to nearby high-quality medical services. Of course, there are still problems in management and administration of rights and duties in the multi-site working policy that will present themselves once it is truly implemented, such as how to deal with and who is responsible for medical malpractice. So the next step is to refine and standardize the policy, and then physicians will be more willing to get involved.

The **Decision** not only affirms the position of the market but also further elevates it from having a basic role to having the decisive role. In the healthcare field, with the deepening of reform, more and more deep-seated contradictions and problems will come up. Encouraging social forces to participate in the medical sector, breaking the monopoly, and permitting competition will accelerate the process of healthcare reform.

4. Improving the Family Planning Policy

He Hui, who does administrative work, is one of the first group of only children born after China implemented the family planning policy. She wanted to give her daughter a brother or sister to play with, and she and her husband had looked forward for several years to the policy of allowing couples to have two children if one parent is an only child. He Hui said that she envied her childhood friends who had brothers and sisters, and hoped to make up for that by giving her daughter a sibling. But the 36-year-old mother Fan Shi said, "Life is too stressful and the cost of raising a child is too high. The prices of milk, healthcare, nursery, education, and so on are increasing. However, with such a policy, people will have a choice as to whether to have the second child." The two mothers in the story are all concerned about an important topic in current China: allowing couples to have two children if one parent is an only child

The **Decision** proposes to adhere to the basic state policy of family planning, to launch the policy of allowing couples to have two children if one parent is a single child, and gradually to adjust and improve the family planning policy so as to promote long-term balanced population development. This policy is referred to as "two children for only children". This policy applies to a family where one parent is an only child, but it does not apply to families who give birth to twins. To make it simple, the family planning policy looks at the number of total children rather than the number of births.

Although the policy of allowing couples to have two children if one parent is an only child is a major adjustment and improvement of the family planning policy, it does not indicate the loosening of the family planning policy. There is no fundamental change in the basic national situation of an overly large population, and China still has the largest population in the world. The pressure of this large population on the economy, society, resources, and environment will still be long-standing, and family planning is still China's basic national policy. In fact, the family planning policy is never unchanging; it has been adjusted and improved in practice. As early as in 1985, Yicheng County in Shanxi Province was specially appointed by the state as the first region to carry out a pilot reform allowing a second child in rural areas, and since then many other counties and cities also did this pilot reform. In 2011, Henan Province implemented the policy allowing couples to have two children if both parents are only children, and later all provinces launched the same policy. And now, the issue of allowing couples to have two children if one parent is an only child is attracting more and more public attention.

Since the beginning of the 21st century, China's population situation has greatly changed. Although having a large population is a basic fact of China, structural problems due to population have become an increasingly important factor affecting economic and social development. Wang Pei'an, deputy director of the National Health and Family Planning Commission, summed up this situation in four points —low birth rates have remained fairly stable with a little decrease, structural problems due to population have become increasingly prominent, family size continues to shrink, and the willingness of the urban and rural residents to have children has changed dramatically. In 2008, the National Health and Family Planning Commission began preparatory work to improve the family planning policy, and organized in-depth research and demonstration, including the final evaluation of the Eleventh Five-Year plan for population development, a survey of birth rates in thousands of villages, an investigation into the marriage and child-bearing conditions of only children in 150 counties, and a nationwide verification of basic information of children ages 0 to 9. It also carried out statistical comparison and verification based on the data provided by education, public security, statistics, and other relevant departments so as to make relatively objective and accurate judgments and estimates about the total population and structure, birth rates, and trends of population movement. On the basis of repeated debate, the 3rd Plenary Session of the 18th CPC Central Committee launched the policy of allowing couples to have two children if one parent is an only child. This policy is a timely adjustment of China's population and family planning policy to adapt to the economic and social development situation, as well as a positive measure to deal with decline in population dividends, labor shortages, and other problems.

The implementation of the policy of allowing couples to have two children if one parent is an only child does not set time limits nationwide, and provinces, autonomous regions, and municipalities can determine their specific time frames according to the actual situation. On November 19th, 2013, after approval by Zhoushan City, the Zhejiang Provincial Government first launched the Zhoushan Island Special Approval Policy–couples can be included in the scope for special approval in family planning if either husband or wife has a family registration in Zhoushan, one is an only child, and the two have only one child.

After the release of the policy of allowing couples to have two children if one parent is an only child, will the population begin to grow rapidly? Firstly, from a nationwide perspective, the total population qualified for the policy is not large–only 20 million or so–and different regions will launch the policy at different times, so a significant short-term increase in population is impossible. Secondly, as pointed out by Yang Yiyong, director of Research Institute for Social Development, National Development and Reform Commission, "Once the new policy is implemented, the effects on birth rate and population structure caused by annual population growth in the millions will be minimal". The intention for relaxing the family planning policy is to satisfy people's desire to have more children and to protect the reproductive rights of these people. Moreover, the policy is gradual. The policy now allows a second child only for a portion of the population, and it is estimated that in around 2030, policies restricting having a second child will be fully relaxed. Third, desire to have a child does not necessarily result in actually reproducing. The results from a survey led by Zhai Zhenwu, dean of the School of Sociology and Demography at Renmin University of China, shows that in a survey with a sample size of nearly ten thousand, only half of the couples who qualified for the second child policy were willing to have a second child. A sample survey conducted in 2012 by the population department in Shanghai shows that there are not many cases where second children are actually born to families qualified for the policy of having a second child if both parents are only children, and the ideal number of children for couples born after 1980 with Shanghai family registration is 1.2. In the cities including Yicheng county in Shanxi, Jiuquan in Gansu, Chengde in Hebei, and Enshi in Hubei, which conducted the pilot reform of the "second child program" in the 1980s, the average ideal number of children was less than 1.6.

China is a populous country. To solve the problems of how to have children, not being willing to have children, and not being able to afford having children, it is not enough just to relax the policy controlling the number of children families can have; it is even more important to make efforts in peak childbirth and improving the distribution of high-quality educational and healthcare resources, and continue to adjust the family planning policy.

Part 6 Social Governance: Innovation and Harmony

In ancient China, floods were rampant and the people suffered. Gun (a mythical figure of prehistoric China) was appointed to do the task of controlling the floods. He stole magical soil from heaven to make dikes to stop the floods, but he failed. His son Yu the Great changed the concept of water control from blocking to draining. Through governing the river courses, he guided the excess water into the sea, and stopped the flooding. This is the famous Chinese legend "Yu the Great Controls the Waters". The 3rd Plenum of the 18th CPC Central Committee for the first time replaced "social management" with "social governance". A difference of a single word shows a shift of governing philosophy.

The nature of society is the relationship between people. A harmonious society which arises in a safe, stable political environment from the orderly interactions between citizens is capable of self-regulation as an organism and can release the greatest vitality and creativity, creating a good environment for politics, the economy, culture, ecology, and other areas, and maintaining the stability of the country as well as promoting the progress and development of society. The Chinese government must handle its relationship with society well in a time of reform and development, keeping full respect for the autonomy and adaptability of the society. It should delegate powers to the society in the fields where it can perform well, constantly innovate governance methods, stimulate social vitality, guide the spiritual growth of citizens, and make sure that society is vibrant, harmonious, and orderly.

Part 6 Social Governance: Innovation and Harmony

1. Improving Governance Methods

Meilong Third Village in the Lingyun Sub-district of Xuhui District, Shanghai, is an old town, inhabited by more than 6,500 people in more than 38 old public houses. The environment of the community is of people's concern as the population is increasing. A few years ago, there were plastic bags and beverage cans everywhere. Now, garbage and waste have been transformed into green chairs and bags, and the clean community looks tranquil and warm. All these changes should be credited to Fang Cuiying and nine other retired housewives. On their own accord, they started an environmental project called the "Green Housewives", aimed at guiding people to change the habit of littering. Due to the community's narrow roads, it is often packed with cars at night and on weekends. Fire engines simply could not get down the road in case of a fire, which was a huge security hazard. The Green Housewife action group submitted a suggestion to the general party branch of the community as well as community committees that they renovate and widen the road. After renovation, the traffic situation has greatly improved. Today, the Green Housewife group has attracted more than 200 people, and nearly 300 families have participated enthusiastically, forming a unique model of community residents' autonomy in Meilong Third Village.

Since the 4th Plenary Session of the 16th CPC Central Committee came up with the goal of building a socialist harmonious society, community building and self-governance in China have developed quickly. For many older Chinese people, "residents committee" is a more familiar term. As early as 1989, the National People's Congress passed the Urban Residents Committee Organization Act of the People's Republic of China, confirming that the residents committee is a grass-roots mass self-governance organization for residents' self-management, self-education, self-service, and self-monitoring.

The residents committee plays an important role in handling public affairs, dealing with public utilities, safeguarding the legitimate rights and interests of residents, and many other aspects. The first reaction of many people when encountering various problems in life is to turn to the residents committee.

However, in the 1980's and 1990's, many residential areas across China were connected with work units. With the construction of commercial housing and the increasing mobility of the population, the original residents committee method gradually was unable to meet the needs of the times in terms of management efficiency and quality. In this context, in accordance with recent development, the government proposed the concept of "community". In 2005, the Ministry of Civil Affairs issued the Opinions on Promoting Urban Community Construction, defining a community as a residents committee adjusted in scale in the community system reform, and proposed that community building should be adapted to urbanization and modernization requirements, to build new communities with regional characteristics and a sense of identity, and to build a new community system. New community committees provide a more relaxed environment for exploring community self-governance. A large number of trained full-time community workers have enhanced the level of community building with more specialized services.

On holidays and festivals, it is very common in cities for communities to organize parties, parent-child communication activities, visits to the elderly, and other services. The community is increasingly becoming a family full of humanity.

In November 2010, the State Council issued the Opinions on Strengthening and Improving the Urban Community Residents Committee. It emphasizes the importance of community autonomy based on the considerable development of community culture, and suggests that community committees should organize residents to participate in public policy hearings in an orderly manner on things concerning their own interests, and conduct self-management activities and related monitoring activities. Action groups such as the Green Housewife project are no longer just a fellowship organization of residents; instead they actively assume the role of mobilizing residents to conduct self-management and supervise community building. Jing'an Community in Zhongnan Road Sub-district, Wuchang District, Wuhan, holds hearings four or five times every month, and invites representatives with various interests to attend and discuss matters ranging from repairing doors, to vehicle management and installing access control on the gate. On August 1st, 2012, as the gate access control system had long been neglected and was in disrepair, resulting in financial and security issues due to unauthorized access, the community committee applied special funds to renovate the gate access control system, and to regulate vehicle management. After the renovation, both residents and vehicles would only be able to gain entrance after swiping a purchased card, but this would increase the inconvenience to a certain extent, so the committee held a hearing for the residents to decide whether to implement it or not. Finally, as the vast majority of people agreed with the plan, the community started the reconstruction project.

On the basis of summing up practical experience in community building and self-government, the **Decision** proposes that "to innovate social

governance systems", the first task is to "innovate social governance methods"; and the government should play a leading role and encourage and support participation of all sectors of society so as to achieve the good interaction with government, social self-regulation, and self-governance by residents. Moving from social management to the proposed social governance reflects the change in governing philosophy of the Communist Party of China and the Chinese government. Traditional "management" focuses on direct management of public affairs by the country and the government, which is somewhat mandatory and is mainly carried out through administrative means; while "governance" stresses the effectiveness of the participation of social forces besides the national government, including social organizations and citizens, diversifying governance methods, and establishing laws, ethics, and institutions. To improve social governance is to change the original top-down management style and form synergistic interaction between the varieties of main forces involved in social governance.

Cheng Enfu, Director of the Department of Marxism at the Chinese Academy of Social Sciences thinks that "social governance" is in accord with "promoting the modernization of national governance system and governance capacity" as proposed in the overall layout of the reform. The word for governance in the Chinese language is made up of two characters, "zhi", meaning stability, and "li", meaning organization. The direction for social governance is to take stability as its basis and organization as its primary method, breaking the government's old habit of handling every detail, emphasizing the leading and coordinating role of the government in the social sphere to guide all sectors of society and all powers with respective responsibilities to participate in affairs of common concern to the public. The government should lessen its functions within set limits; the society should regulate itself in an orderly manner. Taking future community building as an example, the sub-district, as an administrative agency of the local government, should play the role of finding direction, implementing policy, coordinating, and so on. The specific implementation of community-building work should be conducted by community committees in accordance with the actual situations, by which process the committees can fully mobilize residents' enthusiasm for community autonomy and rationalize relationships within the community, with other communities, and between the community and sub-district office, police stations and other low-level state organs.

The **Decision** also proposes to innovate social governance methods by adhering to controlling the source, treating both the symptoms and the disease, and focusing on the essentials, moving in the direction of grid-based management and society-based service, improving the platform for low-level comprehensive service management, reflecting and coordinating the interests and demands of the people in various aspects and at all levels in a timely manner. The mesh governance similar to that in community building has become the basis of "grid management", but in practice, there are still problems of delay in action and insufficient centralization of available methods. The future grid management will truly integrate all forces involved in social governance into a grid, achieve the sharing of information and resources, and improve the level of collaboration and emergency response

capabilities; while also giving full play to the advantages of community organizations which have wide coverage and know the local conditions. It will thereby overcome the deficiencies of individual grid management by creating a comprehensive community service management platform, creating grids within grids, and ultimately realize the goal of social governance to treat both symptoms and root causes.

The 3rd Plenary Session of the 18th CPC Central Committee clearly put forward the decisive role of the market in resource allocation, and "innovating the social governance system" as a way to plan future reforms in the social system is essentially consistent with the concept of the decisive role of the market. Powers are delegated to both the market and society, both giving freedom to the productive forces and social vitality. The logic behind this is that the ultimate manifestation of the fruits of economic development is societal progress.

2. Stimulating Social Vitality

Shaba Elementary School in Huaxi Township, Qianxinan Prefecture, Guizhou Province is located in a poor, mountainous region where transportation is not convenient. 120 of the total 169 students are unable to go home for lunch at noon because the school is too far from their homes. At noon on April 2nd, 2011, the children were lining up in front of the dining hall (converted from a classroom), waiting for their first hot meal at school. Soon, they were sitting together in twos and threes gulping down their food. The hall was permeated with smells of rice and other food. Their warm meals are full of love from society. One month ago, the reporter Deng Fei micro-blogged an appeal for donors for providing free lunch to students in poor areas, which quickly got responses from netizens. Then with the support of the media, the China Social Welfare Foundation, and other social forces, Deng Fei launched the "Free Lunch" program. It adopts the operating pattern of a non-profit organization, takes advantage of e-commerce platforms to raise money, and is managed and supervised by volunteers, caring people, government, media, non-profit institutions and other forces. Shaba Elementary School is the first school supported by the foundation. Now, in the Free Lunch online store, one can make a "donation of love" of 3 *yuan*, click payment and confirmation, and the donation will be sent to the Free Lunch official account. The whole procedure takes less than three minutes. By October 2013, total donations to the Free Lunch Project had reached 68 million *yuan*, providing 350 schools and 75,000 people with free meals across 21 provinces and autonomous regions throughout China.

Since the beginning of the 21st century, China's non-governmental organizations have been developing rapidly, and the Free Meal Project is a typical case. Under the current classification of non-governmental organizations in China, the number of social organizations, private non-profits, and foundations registered with civil affairs departments increased from 142,000, 124,000, and 954 respectively in 2003, to 271,000, 225,000, and 3,029 respectively in 2012. Meanwhile, the structure of non-governmental organizations has also undergone significant changes, with foundations and other sponsored and supported organizations developing rapidly, with private foundations sponsored mainly by entrepreneurs and the rich showing explosive growth. Urban community and social organizations are more active than ever and the trend of Internet-based social organizations is continuing. Public resources focus more on group education, AIDS prevention, disability services, provisions for the elderly, and other community services as well as other public services such as disaster relief.

Social organizations cannot be developed rapidly without reform of administrative management system. For a long time, China imposed a dual management system on private social organizations. A social organization had to get the approval of the managing authorities of its field before it could obtain legal status, and then had to apply for registration with the registration authority of the civil affairs department. This rigid system is not fit for the practical operational needs of increasingly active non-governmental organizations. In 2006, Guangdong Province took the lead in abolishing managing authorities of industry associations through local legislation, a breakthrough in reforming the dual management system of social organizations. In 2008, Shenzhen began to innovate in registration and management system of social organizations, stipulating that industry, business, and economic organizations, social welfare organizations, and charitable organizations would be able to apply directly to the registration authority for registration. Beijing removed the application requirement for organizations on April 1st, 2009. Afterward, the responsible party only had to go to the Society Affairs Office of Beijing Civil Affairs Bureau to register and submit materials; the Society Affairs Office will examine the materials with other departments, and reply within 20 working days. If an organization is qualified, it can immediately enter the registration stage, and no longer needs to rely on managing authorities. In addition, the Beijing government has authorized a number of "hub-type" official organizations, including the Federation of Trade Unions, the Communist Youth League, Women's Federation, Association for Science and Technology, Disabled Persons' Federation, Returned Overseas Chinese Federation, and Literary Federation, to be the "hosts" of new organizations. The government provides capital by purchase of services for these official organizations in order better to manage and serve them.

The attempts made by local governments have provided experience for nationwide reform of the dual management system. In March 2011, China made it clear in the Twelfth Five-year Plan that it would "improve social organization and management, establish and innovate the mechanism of unified registration, with each having its own functions, coordination, grading responsibility and supervision according to law". In 2012, the Ministry of Civil Affairs launched a direct registration procedure for inter-sector and inter-industry social organizations as a new mechanism characterized by unified registration and unified regulation. In March 2013, the State Council issued the Notice of the General Office of the State Council on Dividing Tasks for Implementation of the State Council Plan for Institutional Reform and Functional Transformation, which clarified the direct registration system implemented by civil affairs departments for four types of social organizations; namely, trade associations, science and technology organizations, charity organizations, and urban and rural community service organizations.

From local to national, from part to the whole, the Chinese government has carried out reform of the social organization and management system in a smooth and orderly manner in the past five years, making the role of non-governmental organizations more and more significant in social construction. The **Decision** proposes that stimulating the vitality of social

organizations is an important part of innovating the social governance system. The government should correctly handle its relationship with society, accelerate the separation of the government and society, and encourage social organizations to clarify rights and responsibilities, self-govern by laws, and be useful. Public services and issues within the capacity of social organizations should be provided and resolved by them. Professor Xiang Chunling holds that to stimulate the vitality of social organizations is actively to guide those organizations in playing a synergistic role in social governance, forming a resultant force along with the government, which assumes overall responsibility and decides the direction of social construction.

The **Decision** has clearly expressed the need to develop voluntary service organizations, set time limits for implementing real detachment of trade associations from administrative bodies, and focus on cultivating and developing four types of social organizations. These are trade associations, science and technology organizations, charity organizations, and urban and rural community service organizations, and can directly apply for registration according to law upon establishment. In fact, the deregulation of trade associations and other organizations has gradually made progress in the past five years. The **Decision** re-emphasizes the direct registration of four organizations, reflecting the idea of strengthening guidance on classification of social organizations and developing key organizations. It is necessary to simplify the registration process and lower the threshold for organizations providing direct economic and societal services and offer more development space and greater opportunities, reflecting the shift in management from restricting entrance to encouraging entrance and from administrative control to governance according to law.

With the deepening of the reform and opening up and increasing of foreign exchange, the activities of overseas social organizations in China have been increasing, playing an important role in many areas such as disaster relief and environmental protection. But apart from foreign foundations, there is still a large gap that must be filled in the registration and management of foreign associations and foreign private non-profits. For example, in December 2009, although Yunnan provincial government had issued a series of regulations for management of international NGOs, requiring that they must be documented at the provincial Civil Affairs Department and the Foreign Affairs Department, it did not recognize the legal status of international NGOs. With respect to how to manage activities of overseas social organizations in China properly, drawing on advantages and avoiding disadvantages, the **Decision** proposes to "strengthen management of overseas non-governmental organizations in China and guide them in carrying out activities in accordance with the law." It can be expected that the Chinese government will accelerate the development and improvement of relevant policies and regulations, incorporate overseas non-governmental organizations into management in accordance with law as soon as possible, and guide them in participating in social construction in a suitable way. The government will also develop appropriate laws to guard against illegal actions endangering China's national security and social stability.

3. Properly Handling Contradictions

"If anyone messes with Jiahe's development now, I will mess with him his whole life."

These menacing words were written on a large banner and became the slogan of government demolition projects in Jiahe County, Chenzhou City, Hunan Province in 2004. At that time, more than 7,000 people in Jiahe County were relocated so a large commercial city could be constructed. In order to accelerate the progress of the demolition work, the county government issued documents requiring cadres and teachers to suspend their

work and persuade their relatives to leave, and they would be dismissed or transferred to remote areas if they failed to fulfill these tasks. Two sisters Li Hongmei and Li Xiaochun were both teachers in the county, and their husbands were government officials. As their father was reluctant to sign the demolition agreement, they were both divorced on the same day so their husbands would not be affected.

The abuse of powers by the Jiahe County government attracted great attention from Hunan Province and the central government after being exposed by the media. Wen Jiabao, the then-premier, held a special discussion at the State Council executive meeting about the demolition project and compulsory relocation in Jiahe, and Liu Zhifeng, executive deputy minister of the Ministry of Housing and Urban-Rural Development, said straightforwardly at the meeting that the event had a harmful influence, involving collective abuse of executive power, violating laws and rules, and harming public interests. The State Council immediately sent an investigation team to Jiahe, halting the acts against the people and ordering the Jiahe County Party Committee and Jiahe County government to make profound self-criticism. Meanwhile, the judicial department also intervened. The former county party secretary was dismissed and prosecuted, being subject to legal sanctions. Under the auspices of Liu Zhifeng, Li Hongmei and Li Xiaochun restored their marriages, again on the same day.

The conflict between government and citizens centering on demolition in the Jiahe event, along with tense doctor-patient relationships, misconduct by city inspectors, the widening gap between the rich and the poor, the damaged credibility of the judiciary, and corruption of officials are significant social conflicts in current China. How to deal with these contradictions properly and respond to emergent events endangering social stability correctly has become a social issue facing the central government and local governments. The Decision of the CPC Central Committee on Several Major Issues Pertaining to Building of a Socialist Harmonious Society, deliberated and passed by the 6th Plenum of the 16th CPC Central Committee in 2006, specifies that the building of a socialist harmonious society is an ongoing process of resolving social conflict, and the ruling party needs to have a deep understanding of the class characteristics of China's development, scientifically analyze conflicts and problems impacting social harmony and their causes, more positively face and resolve conflicts, and maximize harmonious factors and reduce disharmonious factors, so as to constantly promote social harmony.

In recent years, many sudden public events center on rural issues, land acquisition and demolition, law enforcement by urban inspectors, environmental protection, and the justice system. This is caused by the lack of channels for smooth expression of public interest, demands, and speech. If the local government does not respond in a timely manner or improperly handles these events, the conflict will be further intensified and turn into unnecessary confrontation. In order to detect, direct, and resolve conflicts early, the Chinese government should gradually reform and improve the administrative appeal mechanism and the system for complaint letters and calls so as to provide the public with smooth and secure channels for expression and establish a conflict relief and risk warning mechanism.

In 2007, on the basis of the Administrative Appeals Law of the People's Republic of China, the State Council formulated the Regulations on Implementation of the Administrative Appeals Law of the People's Republic of China to further standardize the administrative appeal system. Local governments have gradually explored ways to reform this system according to local conditions. Jiangsu Province detailed the policy of adopting hearings for major and complex cases as designated in the Regulations on Implementation, specifying the case types applicable for hearings and the rights of applicants. In the same year, Hubei Province put forward the director responsibility system for administrative appeals, stipulating that

heads of governments and departments at all levels should personally listen to the reports, study the cases, and then inspect and examine them. In 2011 Shanghai carried out pilot work on the administrative appeals committee of city, district, and county level governments, and the committee was led by the government with experts and scholars participating. Reforms in these areas are designed to emphasize administrative appeals as the main channel for resolving administrative disputes, listen to public interest and demands through the monitoring and correction mechanism of the administrative system, and protect their legitimate rights and interests.

As for the reform of complaint letters and calls, the Regulations on Complaint Letters and Calls issued in 1995 is the institutional basis for related work. In 2008, more than 2,800 county committee secretaries nationwide took the lead in receiving visitors, and resolved a number of petitions accumulated over a long time during a short period. In January 2009, the General Office of the CPC Central Committee and the State Council announced the Opinions on Cadres Receiving Calls Regularly, consolidating the successful experiences of cadres receiving complaint visits and upgrading it to a long-term mechanism. On July 1st, 2013, the State Bureau for Letters and Calls fully opened to the public on the Internet for taking complaints. Internet letters and calls have become the preferred way of petition, and the daily amount of letters and calls received is above 1,200. According to statistics, by November 25th, 2013, the State Bureau for Letters and Calls had received 130,172 online complaints, and those with specific demands accounted for 93%. After removing duplicate and invalid complaints, about 95,000 were transferred and assigned by the State Bureau for Letters and Calls to local authorities, and inadmissible complaints were also responded to promptly. Complainants can find the results of their petitions online.

In view of past experience in dealing with social conflicts, the **Decision** has shown there is a necessity to innovate mechanisms to prevent and resolve social conflicts effectively, improve the assessment mechanism for social stability risks caused by major decisions, establish a smooth and orderly mechanism for expression of desires, psychological intervention, conflict mediation, and interests protection so that problems can be reflected on, conflicts can be resolved, and the interests can be protected. Conflicts are inevitable in society, not something to be scared of. The wisdom of the governance of a society can be reflected in its prevention and resolution of conflicts. Professor Xiang Chunling believes that to innovate mechanisms for conflict prevention and resolution can integrate three resources, personal conciliation, administrative conciliation, and judicial conciliation, so as to form a large work pattern.

The **Decision** proposes to reform the administrative appeals system, improve the hearing mechanism for administrative appeals cases, and correct illegal or otherwise improper administrative behavior. The next point of attack in the reform is in strengthening the impartiality and neutrality of the administrative appeals departments and enhancing their authority in resolving administrative disputes. Establishing an independent administrative appeals committee with a diversified committee structure by centralizing and concentrating the administrative appeals rights of various departments, and

adopting the working mode of unified acceptance, centralized investigation, and independent decision to form a new government-led mechanism with professional guarantees and social participation is a reform path that deserves exploration.

With respect to the reform of letters and calls of complaint, the **Decision** requires the implementation of online submission, establishment of a sound and timely mechanism to resolve the reasonable demands of the masses, placement of complaint letters and calls involving litigation or lawsuit within the rule of law, and establishment of a system of settling those complaints legally. According to information disclosed at the press conference held by the State Bureau for Letters and Calls on November 28th, 2013, the Bureau will implement the **Decision** with the principles of smoothness, standardization, openness, and effectiveness. Smoothness means to further open up and broaden channels for complaints, use hotlines, video calls, the post, proxy agencies and other ways to fully implement joint acceptance of complaints and petitions at the city and county levels, and begin to use the Internet as the main channel for resolving complaints. Standardization means to specify the petition system in terms of procedure, content, and order, to improve the ability of staff to act in accordance with law, to further increase regional responsibility, and to actively guide the masses step by step in expressing their demands in a rational and lawful way. Openness means to vigorously implement the "sunshine complaint policy", to increase the transparency of the work, and to publicize through the Internet major procedures of complaint and calls including reception, handling and results. The pilot evaluation system of public satisfaction of handling complaint visits and calls will be fully implemented on November 1st, 2014. In particularly complex complaint letters and calls, public hearings will be held and the process and results will be publicized. Effectiveness is a requirement for the result of complaint letters and calls. In the future, the government will continue to carry out measures for cadres at the city and county levels to receive letters and calls, integrate resources and power to resolve outstanding complaints, carry out re-examination and review work of complaints, improve assessment methods, and encourage the local authorities to focus on the prevention and handling of problems.

4. Protecting Public Safety

In April 2013, new mother Zhang Qian was very worried about her baby's feeding. While on maternity leave, breastfeeding would not be a problem, but nowadays the weaning period of infants is generally longer, and some children as old as three even continue to take milk, powdered milk, or other dairy products as a supplement. After the melamine crisis in infant formula in a number of Chinese dairy corporations, she was not able to trust domestic dairy products. Many of her friends who also have babies often ask others to purchase infant formula from overseas, and Zhang Qian was going to do so as well. Unexpectedly, in January 2013, dairy products imported from New Zealand were found to be contaminated with dicyandiamide. As New Zealand is the source of milk for a lot of international brands of milk powder, Zhang did not know what to do.

Not only dairy products, but many other daily necessities, such as cooking oil, rice, seasonings, etc., have had quality issues in recent years. The food processing industry is one where quality-related problems often occur, and cases of violation of hygienic standards happen frequently. Quality-related problems due to illegal operation by manufacturers and ineffective supervision often arise in the drug industry, which is closely related to each person's health. Food and drug safety has become one of the issues of greatest concern to the Chinese people.

On April 15th, 2012, CCTV Weekly Quality Report reporters found in Xinchang, Zhejiang during a survey that a number of local medicinal capsule manufacturers used industrial gelatin from Hebei and other places. However, to reduce production costs, the suppliers of this raw material purchased cheap leftovers from tanning leather factories to produce their gelatin. According to the *Chinese Pharmacopoeia*, the gelatin used for producing capsules should at least reach the standards for edible gelatin, and industry standards clearly define that edible gelatin must be made from animal skin and bones, and it is prohibited to use any industrial waste from leather tanning. Those capsules produced with industrial gelatin were then sent by reporters for pharmaceutical inspection, and the result was that the chromium content was 20 times the national standard. Xinchang is known for capsule manufacturing in China and has an annual output of around one hundred billion capsules, accounting for about 1/3 of the national output. Usage of these capsules containing dangerous amounts of chromium by pharmaceutical manufacturing companies would bring great risk to users of the medicine produced.

The day after the program was broadcast, the China Food and Drug Administration issued an urgent notice suspending the sales and use of 13 kinds of exposed medicinal capsule products, ordering the affected provinces to carry out supervision, inspection, and testing of chromium content for medicinal capsule products, and dispatching staff to the scene for supervision. The Ministry of Public Security also held a video meeting on April 19th, urging public security organs to actively cooperate with relevant departments to closely investigate and crack down the on the "poison capsule" crimes, and the meeting also organized local public security organs in provinces involved in the investigation. Subsequently, after the investigation by public security organs, 6 cases were filed, 53 suspects were arrested, 10 manufacturers of industrial gelatin and medicinal capsules were shut down, and more than 230 tons of industrial gelatin were inspected and detained on the spot.

Part 6 Social Governance: Innovation and Harmony

Food and drug safety problems causing potential hazard to the public health strike a sensitive nerve in society, which indicates that the ability of law enforcement and supervision of relevant areas needs to be improved. In comparison, sudden natural disasters, which also endanger the public safety, are tests of the emergency response system and the government's ability to mobilize and coordinate. At 8:02 on April 20th, 2013, an earthquake measuring 7.0 on the Richter scale hit Lushan County in Ya'an City, Sichuan Province, and caused extreme damage. Sichuan Province activated Grade 1 emergency procedures immediately after the earthquake, China Earthquake Administration activated its Grade 1 response program for earthquake emergencies, the National Disaster Reduction Bureau and the Ministry of Civil Affairs activated the Grade 3 response program for earthquake relief work, and the Ministry of Public Security, the Ministry of Land and Resources, the China Meteorological Administration, and other departments all used emergency systems to deploy relief workers. Compared to the reaction to the Wenchuan earthquake five years ago, the Chinese government displayed a more mature emergency response system and more efficient disaster relief and social mobilization in its response to the Lushan earthquake. In the face of sudden disasters, the government should minimize losses and protect the public safety in affected areas by means of rapid and rational deployment and action.

Public safety is an important issue for social governance. The **Decision** proposes to establish a sound public safety system, create a unified and authoritative food and drug safety regulatory organization, establish the most stringent regulatory system covering the entire production process, establish systems to trace the origins of food and for labeling of quality to ensure food and drug safety. It is also necessary to deepen the reform of management of safe production, and establish systems of screening for hazardous materials and security prevention and control. Serious accidents must be eliminated and

the disaster prevention and relief system must be improved; comprehensive management of social security must be strengthened, a three-dimensional security and protection system must be created, and all kinds of criminal activities must be strictly guarded against and punished according to law. With respect to new challenges for national security brought about by the Internet, the **Decision** proposes to adhere to the policy of active use, scientific development, management according to law, safety protection, strengthening the management of Internet, and improving the Internet governance leadership structure to ensure national network and information security. For the top-level design of the public safety system, it first proposes the establishment of the State Security Council of the People's Republic of China to improve the national security system and national security strategy so as to ensure national security.

With respect to the establishment of the State Security Council of the People's Republic of China, Professor Gong Fangbin of the People's Liberation Army National Defense University believes that this is a system design based on the existing mechanism and targeted at new situations and problems emerging in the security system. With the changing domestic and international environment, national security is not limited to national defense, military, and diplomatic issues anymore; it is also related to economy, finance, energy, science and technology, information, culture, society, and other fields. The establishment of the State Security Council of the People's Republic of China can better safeguard national security by learning from the experience of other countries, and is suitable to China's new position as a great power. The core mechanism with the State Security Council of the People's Republic of China is for coordination and decision-making; it incorporates functions of different departments such as national defense, foreign relations, intelligence, finance, economy, and trade, carries out overall deployment for the national security system and security strategies. At the highest point in the top-level

Part 6 Social Governance: Innovation and Harmony

design and strategic planning, it will coordinate the specific actions of various sectors to cope with multi-level security challenges in fields such as national defense, economy, finance, information, environment, and terrorism, thus providing maximum protection for the public safety system.

Public safety is the most basic public service provided to citizens by a government, and it is also the fundamental guarantee for the stability and running of society. A society which allows people to enjoy a sense of security can fully mobilize the enthusiasm of its people to participate in social construction and offer advice for social governance, thereby promoting the healthy development of the society. The 3rd Plenary Session of the 18th CPC Central Committee takes the improvement of the public safety system as a fundamental factor to build a secure and harmonious social environment, and guide and promote Chinese society to find the path of development suitable for itself and benefitting the people through in-depth reforms in all areas.